PHILIP TIMMS'
VANCOUVER
1900 – 1910

Fred Thirkell and Bob Scullion

VICTORIA · VANCOUVER · CALGARY

Heritage House Publishing Company Ltd.
#108 – 17665 66A Avenue
Surrey, BC V3S 2A7
www.heritagehouse.ca

Library and Archives Canada Cataloguing in Publication
Timms, Philip T., 1874–1973
    Philip Timms' Vancouver: 1900–1910 / Fred Thirkell and Bob Scullion.

Includes bibliographical references and index.

ISBN-13: 978-1-894974-18-9
ISBN-10: 1-894974-18-2

    1. Timms, Philip T., 1874–1973. 2. Vancouver (B.C.)—History—Pictorial works. I. Thirkell, Fred, 1930- II. Scullion, Bob, 1937- III. Title.

FC3847.37.T566 2006   971.1'33'00222   C2006-905337-5

Edited by Karla Decker
Interior design by Bob Scullion
Cover design by Jacqui Thomas

Photo Credits:
Vancouver Public Library Special Collections: pp. 133 (7698), 134 (7695), 137 (6821), 149 (5132, 5135), 156 (5665), 158 (5773), 165 (6746), 166 (6749), 174–175 (3428)
Vancouver Museum: p. 187 (H 975-184-2)

Printed in Canada

Heritage House acknowledges the financial support for its publishing program from the Government of Canada through the Book Publishing Industry Development Program (BPIDP), Canada Council for the Arts, and the province of British Columbia through the British Columbia Arts Council and the Book Publishing Tax Credit.

TO
A LOYAL FRIEND
AND A BEAUTIFUL COMPANION
NOW SADLY MISSED

MEGAN

1988 – 2006

Acknowledgements

While there are a number of people and institutions we want to thank for their help in connection with *Philip Timms' Vancouver: 1900–1910*, three must be singled out for special mention. First, Lois Peters, Philip Timms' only granddaughter, shared family records that she has laboriously gathered over the years. Without her help we would not have been able to say much about Timms' long and many-faceted life. The other two people who have done so much to make this book possible are Chris McGregor and John Keenlyside. Both men, who have outstanding collections of Philip Timms' postcards, allowed us to select and use the ones from their collections that we felt best represent Timms' stated purpose, which was "to record the city's vistas of the days of its exuberant youth before it was all swept away."

At the Vancouver Public Library, we particularly appreciated the help provided by Andrew Martin of Special Collections. Rosemary Keelan of New Westminster Public Library's Reference Department was most helpful on a number of occasions. At the Vancouver City Archives, both Carol Haber and Megan Schlase have, as usual, provided help beyond the call of duty. The Vancouver Centennial Museum's curator of history, Joan Seidl, and conservator Carol Brynjolfson provided valuable information relating to Timms' favourite camera. Much help regarding film and pictorial tonal quality was provided by David A. Gibson and Mark Osterman of the George Eastman House/ International Museum of Photography and Film in Rochester, New York. To them, and to John Luccock, Margaret Waddington, Don Steele and Albert Tanner, who often pointed us in the right direction as we worked on *Philip Timms' Vancouver: 1900–1910*, we also say "thank you."

At Heritage House we have appreciated the support of Rodger Touchie, our publisher; Karla Decker, our editor; Vivian Sinclair, Heritage House's managing editor; and Susan Adamson and Jacqui Thomas, who know so much about design and layout.

This is our seventh book on old postcards and early photographers of British Columbia. When we produced *Postcards from the Past* back in 1996, we didn't realize we were starting something that was going to become a cottage industry! We want to express particular thanks to our respective spouses, Lil and Beth, who have not only tolerated but encouraged us as our little enterprise has continued on from year to year.

Fred Thirkell and Bob Scullion

Table of Contents

THE MANY LIVES OF PHILIP TIMMS

Philip Thomas Timms was born September 16, 1874, in Toronto, Ontario. The sixth child of George Young Timms and his wife Harriet, Philip was the first of the couple's children to be born in Canada—although his birthplace did not alter the fact that his attitudes, loyalties and industrious nature very much reflected the values of a family that, for the most part, was English-born and bred.

The Timms family had lived in Oxfordshire longer than anyone could prove to the contrary. George Timms, born October 19, 1842, was indentured to an Oxford printer and became a journeyman compositor in May 1862. By law, an apprentice was prohibited from competing with a former master, so Timms moved to London in 1862, where he opened his own shop.

Life was difficult in London, and not long after marrying Harriet Hodiah Harris on October 31, 1863, he set off for New York to look into opportunities for work as a journeyman printer. New York was not to his liking—he missed the old flag and the British way of life—so he moved on to Ottawa, which in those days had little to offer but seemingly endless winters. He then pressed on to Toronto, where he got a job as a foreman in a printing house. Having secured good, permanent employment, he sent for his family to join him.

That family was large. Although their daughter Lois Maria had only lived 10 months, the Timms' four other children accompanied Harriet and her parents, Thomas and Harriet Harris, aboard the Allan Steamships' new immigrant ship, *Circassian,* arriving in Quebec City on August 10, 1873. The family moved to Toronto and settled quickly into life there. The Timms children, George Frederick (Fred), Esther Matilda, Gertrude Harriet (Gertie) and Arthur Hubert (Art), born in 1864, 1866, 1868 and 1872

respectively, were joined by four more: Philip Thomas arrived on the scene in 1874; Ethel Charlotte, who only lived for one month, in 1876; Vivian Richard in 1878; and Edward (Ted) James, who was born in 1880.

Initially, George Timms' prospects looked good in Toronto. The local clergy had formed an association, and they needed a printer who could produce not only their Sunday leaflets and other publications, but also their sheet music. Timms was well qualified, having apprenticed in a house that specialized in music publication. The churches did not have a suitable space for offices, presses, storage and so forth, so they agreed that Timms should borrow the money to start a business—known as the Oxford Press—and their association would repay his loan on a regular schedule. Timms became the first music printer in Canada. Unfortunately, the clergy did not keep to their end of the bargain, leaving Timms to fend for himself.

Flat broke, Timms turned to farming. He acquired a homestead in the Muskoka district, near Bracebridge, but the land on it was about as bad as it could be: all it seemed to grow were rocks and boulders. The family promptly christened the farm "Land O' Rocks," and it wasn't long before family members were looking elsewhere for security and income. (Gertrude had already married Bill Seip in Toronto in 1892, thus avoiding the joys of country life.)

By 1894, even though he was only 20 years old, Philip Timms had decided to leave the Land O' Rocks and open a shop in Bracebridge, calling his business "P. T. Timms & Co., Picture Frames, Music, and Stationery." Timms had both training and insight. After finishing school, he had managed to find work as a compositor in the music printing and publishing business, preparing the type for anthems and hymn books. He did well; he was a good student and a fast learner. Like the rest of his family, he was very musical, so he joined one of the local church choirs, and before long was made choirmaster. The church organist, with whom he had to work closely, was a young single lady named Lizzy (never, ever "Elizabeth"!) Maud Slater. She and Philip hit it off, and they were married on September 1, 1897.

Around this time, Philip's two older brothers, Fred and Art, had set off for the west coast. The economy in eastern Canada was not that strong, and talk of gold strikes in the Klondike had a magical appeal for a lot of young men uncertain about their futures. Fred and Art reached Vancouver, which proved to be their Shangri-La. Seeing promising business opportunities there, they put aside thoughts of the Yukon, and lost no time convincing the rest of the family to sell up and make their way to the land of milk and honey. Lizzy was not too keen on the idea, but finally she agreed, and she and Philip joined the family's trek west in 1898. Two or three years later, Gertrude and Bill Seip also made their way to Vancouver.

Philip's brother Fred had opened a print shop of his own, and their father was operating a printing press in a bedroom at home. In his spare time, Art, who worked at a local paper called *The Ledger*, drummed up business for their father's "bedside press."

According to an 1899–1900 Vancouver city directory produced by Rowland E. Green, Philip Timms was employed in S.J. Thompson's Studio and Art Gallery at 616 Granville Street and lived at 234 East 5th Avenue. Thompson was an outstanding photographer whose high-quality platinum photos of the Rockies and Selkirks taken along the CPR right-of-way were sold widely. Thompson also sold original art and cameras, provided a picture-framing service and generously made darkroom facilities available for free to amateur photographers. While Timms' experience as a framer probably got him his paying job, he was no doubt happy to take full advantage of the learning opportunities that working for Thompson provided.

In 1900 Lizzy was pregnant with their first and, as it turned out, only child. She wouldn't even consider having her child born in Vancouver, so she and Philip went back to Bracebridge for Harold Philip's birth on September 21, 1900.

Back in Vancouver in late October, Timms was again in need of a job. It is known that he worked for two or three years for the Edwards Brothers, and it may have been at this time that he began his employment with them.

George and Herbert Edwards had come to Vancouver from Waterloo, Ontario, and opened their business on Cordova Street in 1891; it soon became one of the city's most prestigious firms. Philip doubtless kept his eyes and ears open, adding as much as he could to his knowledge of photography. After work, he would take his camera, get on his bike and pedal off to document life in the city.

In Stanley Park one day, he had come across three men clearing land with a team of horses. He took their pictures, made $15 and decided that the photographer's life was the life for him. Philip felt he had three things going for him: his formal training as a printer, the skills he had acquired in composing and developing good pictures, and the sales experience he had picked up at the ripe old age of 20 in his shop in Bracebridge.

Most importantly, early on in his life in Vancouver Philip Timms recognized, as he later put it, the need "to record the city's vistas of the days of its exuberant youth before it was all swept away." Given that so many of the buildings erected between 1900 and 1910 rarely lasted more than

40 years before they were razed and replaced by "bigger and better" ones, Timms' foresight was remarkable and significant. Certainly other photographers were taking pictures of the burgeoning "Liverpool of the Pacific," but Timms was the only one who deliberately set out to produce a photographic record of Vancouver and its neighbouring municipalities in the opening years of the 20th century. Fortunately, the golden age of Vancouver's youth coincided with the golden age of the picture postcard, when literally billions of postcards were produced throughout the western world for the millions of people who were sending each other "just another view for your album."

In late 1903, Art Timms opened a shop on the northwest corner of Georgia and Hornby that specialized in printing and engraving. In 1904 he invited Philip, by then a struggling, self-employed postcard photographer, and their brother-in-law Bill Seip, who worked as a picture framer and general factotum, into the business. The shop was known as the "Art Emporium." (In later years, Art owned and managed western Canada's largest printing house.)

By the time the Art Emporium opened, Philip was well on his way to compiling his unique photo archive. Even though the Vancouver Public Library has approximately 3,000 Timms negatives, at least half of which were originally printed as picture postcards, there is no way of knowing for certain the exact number of photographs, lantern slides and stereopticon views he produced.

Although trained in printing and best remembered for his photography, Philip Timms was something of a Renaissance man, with interests stretching far beyond these fields and into the realms of science, nature and natural history. He had a special love for Stanley Park, with its many old-growth trees, and considered it "everyone's estate." He visited Siwash Rock annually to photograph it so that he might record the effects of wind and sea on the ancient landmark. He was interested in anthropology and local geology, especially glacial erratics—boulders that are "glacial" because a glacier pushed them from their place of formation to their present location, and "erratic" because they don't match the other types of rock where they are found.

His interest in anthropology was piqued on one occasion when he was lucky enough to be the right person at the right place at the right time. In 1908 he was photographing Eburne and Marpole when he came upon a road crew cutting a right-of-way through the Great Fraser Midden. Timms noticed workmen raking up piles of human bones to fill a hole. Looking around, he discovered the full skeletal remains of a woman, along with tools and other artifacts, dating back over 2,000 years.

Timms' love of animals led him not only to active membership in both the SPCA and the Anti-Vivisectionist Society, but also to become a lifelong vegetarian: for some time he was secretary of the Vancouver Vegetarian Society. (It may have been a visit to a slaughterhouse when he was 27 years old that inspired him to adopt vegetarianism.)

Timms' concern for the environment prompted him to become a member of the Vancouver Natural History Society. Not surprisingly, he became the society's official photographer, and he particularly enjoyed its annual camp-outs on Mount Garibaldi, always taking along his homemade, trailside darkroom and a small, portable "daylight press." The society recognized his contributions in March 1950, when it made him a life member.

Timms garnered several honours over the years. In 1936 he became an Associate of the Royal Photographic Society of Great Britain. He was also a member of the Royal Society of Arts and for years had also been a member of Canada's Royal College of Organists. In 1960 the board of trustees of the Art, Historical and Scientific Association of Vancouver, which had founded and operated the Vancouver City Museum, honoured Timms with a life membership; Timms had been the museum's official photographer for many years.

As far as participation in community life was concerned, Timms knew only one real disappointment. He had badly wanted to become the city's first archivist, but this was not to be; that

The Timms' Homestead Near Bracebridge
The soil was so poor the family called the place "Land O' Rocks."

Bracebridge, 1894
The dapper 20-year-old Philip Timms stands in front of his Bracebridge picture-framing, music, and stationery shop. The young lad is possibly Philip's youngest brother, Ted.

position went to Major J. S. Matthews in 1933.

Matthews' strengths were with documents and records, while Timms' forte was in the photographic record of the city's growth and development. While the two men's interests were in many ways complementary, their relationship was always more professional than cordial. That Timms donated his immense collection of negatives to the Vancouver Public Library rather than to a seemingly more appropriate institution such as the Vancouver City Archives, may say something about the perspectives and working relationship of the two. A member of Philip Timms' family has speculated that perhaps the reason Timms was considered less qualified for the position was that while Matthews had the pension of a retired major and easy access to many of Vancouver's prominent families, Timms had to make a living and would have had less time to give to the job.

Music played a significant role in the lives of Philip Timms and his family. Of five boys and two girls who survived to adulthood, all but one became proficient musicians, each playing several instruments. Their father George was an accomplished musician who particularly enjoyed playing the cello, and had been organist and choirmaster in at least two Anglican parishes in Toronto. As soon as he was old enough, Philip, along with his older brothers Fred and Arthur, became a choirboy—first at St. Matthias, and later at St. Thomas's, both of which his father served as "master of the music."

Brother Fred, like Philip, was a master of sight-reading, and he became organist and choirmaster at Toronto's St. Alban's Cathedral. Later, in Vancouver, he played the oboe, saxophone and cornet in the Mount Pleasant Band under the direction of his youngest brother, Ted.

In the 1920s Ted, his family and his parents, George Young and Harriet Hodiah, moved to Langley, where he opened a theatre; he did vaudeville turns, and his wife played the piano for the silent movies. Eventually, he owned theatres in Abbotsford and White Rock, in addition to the one in Langley; all went well until the Great Depression hit in 1929.

Younger brother Vivian left the Land O' Rocks at age 17, sailing to Britain in 1895 on his way to India. He never got to India, however. Two things changed his plans: one was his attractive cousin, Edith, daughter of his father's brother, Walter, with whom he was staying in Oxfordshire; the other was the Boer War—he had enlisted in the First Oxfordshire Regiment of Light Infantry and when war broke out, he was shipped off to South Africa. During the war, he was in the battle of Paardeburg and also participated in the relief of Kimberley. After the war ended, he returned to Britain and married Edith, and they joined the rest of the family in 1903. In Vancouver he became band sergeant for the Irish Fusiliers and later a member of the "Caribou (*sic*) Cowboys," who were popular on local radio stations.

Sister Esther Matilda was as capable as any of her siblings. An accomplished milliner and dressmaker, she was also a talented pianist and organist. Later in life, she taught piano. Although gifted, however, she was also manipulative. As a young girl, she managed to have her sister Gertrude made responsible for washing the clothes and doing the floors: a budding musician, Esther didn't feel she should have to use her delicate hands for the more mundane aspects of housekeeping. At the advanced old age of 29, still a spinster, Esther agreed to an arranged marriage to her cousin, Edmond Firth. Although she always considered her health to be delicate, she lived to be 97 years old.

Philip's musical accomplishments were in keeping with those of the other family members. As a violinist, he played in the Vancouver Philharmonic Society's orchestra. He also played trombone in Cope's City Band, and in the Vancouver Musical Society's orchestra. He sang in St. James' choir in 1898, the year he arrived in Vancouver, until he became choirmaster at St. Michael's on Broadway, just east of Main. (Rather strangely, the choir's instrumental accompaniment was provided by a cornet). In 1907 Philip, like

The Art Emporium
The flat-roofed building on the left was the Art Emporium, which opened in 1903. It was jointly owned by Philip Timms, his brother Art, and their brother-in-law Bill Seip.

93. The West End.
Vancouver, B. C.

A Store of His Own.
Philip Timms opened his own shop in 1906. Located at 944 Granville Street, it also provided accommodation for the family.

Siwash Rock
Timms visited Siwash Rock annually to record changes wrought by tides and weather. Pictured near the rock are Philip's wife Lizzy and their son Harold.

brother Fred, was also playing in the Mount Pleasant Band led by their youngest brother Ted.

Philip helped raise funds for the formation of the Vancouver Citizens' Band, and acted as its bandmaster, until the workload became too great. In this band, he also played the E-flat bass helicon, a brass wind instrument invented in 1875. The helicon never really caught on and soon disappeared from the musical scene. The Citizens' Band went on to become the band of the 72nd (Seaforth) Highlanders.

It is difficult to imagine that anyone could have as many avocations as Philip Timms; still, the list goes on. One of his passions was education. Not only did he talk about it, he provided it through lectures illustrated with lantern slides that he had created. (And he was generous. If a church or community group wanted him to host an evening, and he felt the sponsoring body's goals were worthwhile, Timms would prepare handbills or posters, print tickets that the organization could sell, and then present one of his illustrated lectures, all at no cost to the sponsors.)

One program he presented was entitled "Our City and its History." Delivered in two parts, the first evening covered the geophysics, or prehistory, of the Lower Mainland, while the second dealt with the Stone Age, early exploration, and White settlement. Another program Timms presented during the Second World War considered "The Evaluation of Vancouver: From the Horse and Buggy Days to Metropolis." He also fostered what he called his "home university and archives," which promoted the collection of artifacts and pictures relating to Vancouver's earliest days. This concept was an Edwardian version of those museum precursors, the "cabinets of curiosities." Eventually much of this collection was presented to the Vancouver Museum.

Considering Timms' volunteer roles, whether in connection with music, archeology, natural history or a number of other fields, one may wonder how he ever found the time to make a living. Nonetheless, he did.

As mentioned earlier, when he first arrived in Vancouver in 1898, he worked with S.J. Thompson and then later at Edwards Brothers, a job he stayed with for several years. A look at Vancouver's city directories for the years 1898 through 1903 offers a few clues about his work history and, at the same time, an idea of the family's frequent moves.

Henderson's 1898 directory shows Philip, Lizzy and other family members living at 653 Barnard Street. In 1899 Philip, Lizzy and other relatives lived at 442 East 6th Avenue—according to Henderson, that is; according to Green's directory, they lived at 234 East 5th. City directories were less than infallible! Philip is also listed as a photographer sharing office space with his brother Fred, a printer, at 517 Seymour Street. The 1902 and 1903 city directories show Philip and Lizzy living at 3014 Westminster Avenue (now 15th and Main), which was Philip's parents' address. He still worked at Edwards Brothers at this time.

In 1904 Philip, Lizzy and young Harold were living at 133 Robson Street, and Philip was listed in the directory as a photographer. (At that time, he was working at the Art Emporium.) In 1906 Philip struck out on his own, opening a shop at 944 Granville, between Smythe and Nelson. He, Lizzy and Harold also lived at this address until 1908, when they moved to 1073 Howe Street. In 1909 Philip moved his shop to 501 West Georgia Street, and his family to 829 East 2nd Avenue. People moved a lot in those days!

In the years before the First World War, it was not difficult for Philip to make a good living as a postcard photographer and, at the same time, work toward his declared goal, to record the life and growth of Vancouver between 1900 and 1910. Timms sold his cards through drugstores, corner stores and shops that attracted the tourist trade. In 1912 the family moved yet again, this time to 1608 Commercial Drive, where he operated his business from home.

By 1913 Philip appears to have given up

1842 Charles Street

Fortunately, the Timms' home at 1842 Charles Street was large. Not only did it house the family, it also had enough space for Philip's vast collections, as well as his Alpha Press, photo lab and "home university."

The Home University

Philip Timms was a strong supporter of continuing education, believing that learning was a lifelong process. He encouraged others to do as he had done, that is, find room in their homes for what we would today call a learning centre. He used space in his basement for displays and for a classroom/theatre.

commercial photography as his primary source of income. In that year, there was a general depression, the postcard craze was waning and he had successfully completed his intended project, photographing Vancouver and its people between 1900 and 1910. He may have felt that he needed to find a more reliable source of income. Whatever the reason, he went to work for his brother Art as a printer/compositor.

Art Timms had learned the printing trade working for his father in Toronto. After coming to Vancouver in 1898, he had further developed his skills working at *The Ledger* and later managing the "Art Emporium." In 1909 he established his own commercial printing house at 14th Avenue and Main Street. In addition to being a good printer, he was also a hard-working, perceptive and insightful businessman. His printing house, in which he had initially invested $2,500, grew into a building and plant that he sold upon retirement in 1942 for $225,000.

Over the years almost every Timms family member worked for Art. Philip was with the firm from 1913 until 1942; from 1913 to 1932 he worked there as a printer/compositor, and from 1933 to 1942 he managed the company's downtown branch office at 418 West Pender.

When Art retired, Philip acquired the branch operation and renamed it the "Alpha Press." By 1946 he had moved the business to his home on Charles Street; the rent for the Pender Street shop was just too high. While Philip had long since ceased to be a full-time commercial photographer, he did continue to do some work in this field.

Around the time of Philip and Lizzy's golden wedding anniversary—September 1, 1947—it was becoming apparent that Lizzy's health was declining. The situation was fast approaching the point where she could not be left alone, and 1947 was the last year that Philip took part in a Natural History Society weekend.

In the early 1950s Lizzy was diagnosed as being in the early stages of what we now know as Alzheimer's disease. Within a decade—by the time of their diamond wedding anniversary—

Lizzy could do no more than be photographed with Philip and the family. To make matters worse, their only son Harold died of cancer on September 16, 1957, a day before his father's 83rd birthday. Not long after, Harold's widow, Hanna, had to spend three years in Pearson TB Hospital. And on October 18, 1957, Lizzy died of Alzheimer's complicated by acute influenza.

In spite of all these sad and life-changing events, Philip decided to continue living in his Charles Street home of 42 years, and his sister Gertrude (Gertie) agreed to come live with him. Gertie was a remarkable and unusual woman. After divorcing her first husband, Bill Seip, she had remarried, and although her second marriage was relatively short—her second husband died after four years—it was both happy and fulfilling. Since she needed to have an income when she was on her own again, she went to work in private homes as a practical nurse.

Gertie was the only member of the family who could not play an instrument, but she had a buoyant and commanding personality, with a passion for social justice; in her youth, she had been an active suffragette. Her beliefs led her to support Tim Buck and the Communist Party, as well as Tommy Douglas and the Canadian Commonwealth Federation. She also supported the outreach programs of the local labour unions, and became one of the founders of Camp Jubilee for the children of the city's economically disadvantaged. (Situated on Indian Arm, Camp Jubilee is still actively fulfilling its original mandate.)

Gertie lived happily with Philip, but the arrangement didn't last. She fell down the stairs, broke a hip and could no longer look after him. At 84, Philip was finding life increasingly difficult to manage. His home was full of memories, and memorabilia: his home university and archives, with all its artifacts and curios, all sorts of musical instruments, a complete printer's shop, a photo lab, photographs, tinted glass slides and stereopticon views, and thousands of glass negatives.

To complicate matters still more, he was not

Postcards Galore

An interior view of Timms' shop at 944 Granville Street. Note the impressive collection of photographic postcards on the wall. Having one of each would be a collector's dream.

In the Basement

In 1913 Philip Timms moved his photo-processing shop to his home. He then worked as a printer/compositor in his brother Art's printing shop, and continued working for him for the following 29 years.

very strong—57 years of vegetarianism may have contributed to his weakened condition—and he had a series of severe nosebleeds. He believed he was a "blood maker," someone who has too much blood. When he got a nosebleed, he just let the bleeding go on; at least once he lost so much blood he lost consciousness.

Diagnosed with acute anemia, he went to the hospital for the first time in his life. After his stay there, he was put on monthly injections of vitamin B-12; the shots gave him a new lease on life. He went to live with his granddaughter Lois and her husband Jim Peters before returning to his home on Charles Street.

In 1960, at the age of 86, Philip's health was such that he could no longer live alone, and again he went to live with Lois and her husband. To accommodate him and his treasures, the couple added four rooms to their home. Before long, Philip had given his irreplaceable collection of glass negatives to the Vancouver Public Library for its newly formed Northwest Room collection. (The value was, of course, well-known.) In 1968 he donated his folding Gundlach-Manhattan Optical Company camera—his favourite—to Vancouver's Centennial Museum. Manufactured in Rochester, New York, in 1902, it was an amazingly portable camera, even though it used fragile, cumbersome 5-by-7-inch glass plate film.

Philip Timms had done exactly what he had set out to do, that is, chronicle nearly every aspect of life in Vancouver between 1900 and 1910 for posterity. And he lived long enough for others to recognize the value of his unique record.

In 1970, Vancouver's library, city archives, and Centennial Museum staff chose 150 of Philip Timms' postcards that they thought would be of greatest interest to the public, and created a one-man show that toured B.C. A catalogue, *Vancouver: the Golden Years*, was produced in conjunction with the exhibition. The catalogue provided an attractive overview of Timms' unique record of Vancouver and the Lower Mainland in the years prior to the First World War.

Philip stayed with Lois and Jim until 1965, when he again decided it would be best if he lived on his own. He moved to an apartment at 1305 Commercial Drive, where he stayed for three years. In 1968, at the age of 94, he stayed first with his grandson Lawrie for seven months, and then again with Lois and Jim for five months. He then tried living on his own once more, this time in a Granville Street hotel. By the fall of 1970, however, it was clear that while he found it difficult to live with others, no matter how caring or accommodating they were, it was no longer possible for him to live independently. Between September 1970 and September 1972 he resided, with difficulty, in three different seniors' facilities. After suffering a stroke in late 1972, he was moved to Fellburn Private Hospital in Burnaby, where he died on August 8, 1973.

On July 21, 1970, Joan Lowndes, the *Vancouver Sun*'s art critic, wrote of the Centennial Museum's show that she hoped "*Vancouver: The Golden Years*" would lead to the production of a publication that would cover … more than the decade 1900–1910, which Philip Timms recorded so fully and beautifully." We hope this book will fulfill that wish, placing Philip Timms and his golden decade in the broader context of his multi-faceted life in the city of his dreams: Vancouver.

On the Trail

Philip Timms loved the outdoors, and nothing gave him more pleasure than the Vancouver Natural History Society's annual camping trips to Mount Garibaldi. Timms took along his portable darkroom (pictured below) so he could quickly develop and print his pictures.

At Home

Even in the years when photography was no longer his vocation, it continued to be his main hobby. He always worked hard to produce outstanding photographs.

Travelling On

Amazingly, in 1958, at the age of 84, Philip Timms went to England on his own. He had never before visited his parents' homeland.

THE CPR COMES TO VANCOUVER

Having been promised a rail connection to central Canada, British Columbia became a province of the Dominion of Canada in 1871. After significant financial and engineering challenges had been overcome, the Canadian Pacific Railway's line was finally completed to tidewater at Port Moody. Amid great rejoicing, the first passenger train from the east arrived on July 4, 1886.

As far back as 1881, however, the CPR's management knew that the harbour at Port Moody, which is at the head of Burrard Inlet, would become too cramped to accommodate the volume of shipping anticipated in years to come. It also knew that there was a small community 12.9 miles farther west on the south shore of the Inlet—a place popularly called Gastown, but officially known as Granville—that would be able to provide an adequate number of docks and anchorages for the many trans-Pacific steamships that would soon be calling regularly at Canada's western railway terminus. Among these ships would be vessels owned and operated by the CPR itself.

Since the federal government and the CPR agreed that Port Moody was to be the Pacific terminus, money for building farther west had to come from a source other than Ottawa. To solve the problem, the railway company secretly entered into negotiations with British Columbia's provincial government for Crown land in what is now Vancouver. The province agreed to a grant of 6,000 acres, half the amount the railway had hoped to receive.

Local large landowners like "The Three Greenhorns"—John Morton, Sam Brighouse and William Hailstone—who had pre-empted 550 acres in what was to become the CPR's (and Vancouver's) exclusive West End, were prevailed upon to "help out" and "donate" one-third of their holdings to the railway company, as a way of assuring the future value of the remaining two-thirds of their pre-emptions. Even though the railway knew it had no choice but to build its line into the area that would later become downtown Vancouver, those who were invited to donate land couldn't be sure. All they knew for certain was that if the railway did not get built through to what is now Coal Harbour, their holdings would be of relatively little value. Better half a cake than no cake at all!

All was not clear sailing, however. When a number of highly incensed Port Moody landowners learned that the railway was to go on to Vancouver, they tried by legal means to prevent it from crossing their lands, which happened to lay across the only practical route for the extension of the line. As it turned out, Canada's highest court decided in favour of the CPR, and construction was allowed to proceed.

Having won its case in court, the CPR lost no time in building its line through to the newly incorporated City of Vancouver. Its first passenger train arrived there amid great fanfare on May 23, 1887. Initially the company's facilities were modest. Thomas Sorby, a well-regarded, British-trained local architect, designed a station, a freight shed and other necessary structures.

While these frame buildings were only intended to serve for a very few years, they were used for over a decade, even though the foundations for a large brick-and-stone station were in place by 1892. Because Vancouver was still a relatively small community and a financial depression was developing in the early 1890s, the railway had second thoughts about spending a lot of money on a new station.

By 1897, however, both Vancouver's and the railway's futures were looking better, and construction of the city's second station was resumed. It was built in the Château style and featured a steep-pitched roof with two impressive towers—one round and one octagonal—above a massive arched entranceway. The design was essentially that of Edward Colonna, who had worked with Bruce Price, the New York architect who had designed the CPR's Château Frontenac and its hotels at Banff and Lake Louise. Colonna had also worked with Louis Comfort Tiffany in New York as a designer, and was noted for his Art Nouveau creations. He had in fact designed parlour and sleeping car interiors for the railway before he was asked to provide the architectural drawings for Vancouver's station. Unfortunately, when the project was reactivated in 1897, Colonna was no longer available to act as supervising architect: he was in Scotland working on the interior design for a steamship being built for the CPR. Colonna's design was enlarged and reworked by Edward Maxwell, another architect who was frequently

At the Foot of Granville Street
While Timms' 1909 postcard is actually featuring the city's new and as yet unfinished post office, the CPR's train station can be seen at the north end of the street. It opened in 1899 and faced onto Cordova Street. While it had great eye appeal, it was soon too small and was replaced in 1912–14 by the much larger neoclassical station known as "Waterfront" that serves today as the downtown SkyTrain terminal.

employed by the railway. Unfortunately, today it is Maxwell, not Colonna, who is generally credited with the station's unique and imaginative design.

Ironically, by the time the station opened in 1899, it was already too small to handle the amount of daily rail traffic moving in and out of Vancouver. Because there was no practical way the building could be enlarged, it had to be razed and replaced by a totally new structure. That third station, built between 1912 and 1914, now serves as the waterfront terminal for Vancouver's SkyTrain system.

Grand Design

Even though the foundation for the CPR's first permanent Vancouver station had been put in place in 1892, adverse economic conditions forced the railway to postpone further construction until 1898.

The building's unique design was the creation of Edward Colonna. As the postcard clearly illustrates, the station, with its steep-pitched roof and massive brick towers atop a 42-foot wide arched entranceway built of stone, was very much in the Château style. While the original design was Colonna's, it was refined and enlarged by Edward Maxwell, who is more often that not credited with being the station's architect.

While the main floor was occupied by ticket offices, waiting rooms and other facilities designed to serve the travelling public, company offices filled the building's upper seven floors. The Land Department occupied the west wing, while the offices of the treasurer and the purchasing agent were in the larger east wing. Executive and general offices were located in the building's centre section.

While not clearly evident in Timms' postcard, Granville Street between Cordova and Hastings was paved with Australian gumwood blocks—the city's first. There were "test sections" of local fir, spruce and cedar, but the local softwoods did not wear well. Whatever kind of wood they were made of, all these end-grain blocks must have been treacherously slippery when wet.

365 LAND BUYERS' ALL NIGHT VIGIL
VANCOUVER, B. C.

The CPR Cashes In

The wet and uncomfortable-looking crowd of men—and a few women—are lined up waiting for the CPR's Land Office to open on April 28, 1909. Many of them had been waiting since early morning to be among the first to buy lots in the CPR's new and exclusive residential district advertised as Shaughnessy Heights.

All homes built in the new subdivision, as a condition of sale, had to cost a minimum of $6,000 at a time when the average city home cost about $1,000. They also had to be single-family dwellings and lots could not be subdivided. The development was more exclusive than heaven: in most instances the deeds of sale contained a restrictive covenant prohibiting the sale of lots to Jews or "Orientals."

Shaughnessy Heights was the brain-child of Richard Marpole, superintendent of the railway's western district. He had proposed its development in 1907. When the CPR attempted in 1914 to have Shaughnessy recognized as a separate municipality—it was part of Point Grey at the time—the provincial government rejected the company's proposal.

A Glimpse of the City.
Vancouver, B. C.

The City's First Freight Yards

The CPR's first local freight yards stretched along Vancouver's waterfront, which soon became lined with wharves and piers. South of the tracks, Water and Alexander streets quickly became home to wholesalers and warehouses. It wasn't until around 1910 that a second wholesale district came into being; it embraced Beatty, Mainland and the south end of Homer Street (CPR lands), which were conveniently served by railway spurs. Still, more space was needed for freight arriving in the Terminal City, as Vancouver was popularly called at the time, and in 1912 the CPR developed extensive freight yards in Coquitlam.

In the opening decade of the 21st century, the land once occupied by the CPR's original waterfront freight yard is being redeveloped without pause, as are other highly desired downtown properties. Some feel the face of the city is being marked or scarred by overly rapid and often mindless redevelopment. They may be right, or they may be wrong—only time will tell.

"Waiting for You."
Vancouver, B. C.

A Time of Anticipation

Timms' picture of waiting hotel buses, hacks and perhaps one or two privately owned carriages must have been taken in the late morning: the *Imperial Limited*'s baggage cars, coaches, dining and observation cars are still standing in the station facing west. The train was likely soon backed up to where it could be moved across Powell, Cordova and Hastings streets, near Carrall Street, and on to the Yaletown yards, where it would have been serviced before returning to the station with its rolling stock in reverse order, ready for the trip back to Montreal. In 1932 a tunnel, now used by SkyTrain, eliminated at last the need for the CPR's engines and railcars to cross busy downtown streets a number of times each day.

The horse-drawn carriages (and perhaps one or two motorized vehicles) are waiting for steamship passengers. It is impossible to say whether they are awaiting the arrival of one of the CPR's *Princesses* that served the coast, or one of the company's trans-Pacific *Empresses* arriving from the Far East. Regardless, there would have been excitement in the air, travel not being so everyday and ho-hum as it is for many people today.

The fact that Timms would be moved to take a picture of the drivers and their hacks, hotel buses or carriages says something not only about his ability to spot a unique subject for a photo, but also about his sensitive interest in the city's people—a trait that made him a popular figure throughout his life.

BARNET

In 1889 James MacLaren, a highly successful Ottawa Valley lumberman and sawmill owner, and Frank Ross, a leading Quebec lumber merchant, purchased timber rights covering 90,000 acres in the upper Fraser Valley and on northern Vancouver Island.

Because B.C. government regulations required those who held provincial timber rights to operate a sawmill within the province for at least six months of every year, MacLaren and Ross built two sawmills in B.C. One was above New Westminster on the Fraser, while the other was at Barnet on Burrard Inlet. The mill on Burrard Inlet was incorporated on June 17, 1889, as the North Pacific Lumber Company. The mill site was on the CPR's main line, 4.4 miles west of Port Moody and 8.5 miles east of downtown Vancouver. MacLaren and Ross initially purchased 120 acres that straddled the CPR's tracks. The mill was built between the tracks and the waterfront, while the residential community was built to the south and above the railway's right-of-way.

The community was named "Barnet," James MacLaren's wife's maiden name. It was also the middle name of MacLaren's son, James Barnet MacLaren, who was actively involved in setting up the mill and served as its business manager. When it came into production in 1891, the North Pacific mill was considered to be one of the best on the coast. Employing 190 men, it could produce 100,000 board feet of lumber, plus shingles, laths and other wood products daily. Unfortunately, in 1893 a worldwide economic depression forced the owners to mothball the mill until 1899, by which time conditions had improved

sufficiently to make reopening it economically viable. And business was good. In 1902 over 25 million board feet of lumber and 30 million shingles were produced and sold.

When the mill reopened in 1899 the community immediately had a population of 150 men, all of whom were housed in dormitories. It took time for proper homes to be built to accommodate those who were married and had families. As might be expected, the homes of the mill manager and senior staff were large and situated on spacious grounds. They were the first buildings to be seen by visitors who approached Barnet by way of its main entrance, which was on the west. Toward the east, cottages for the workmen with families were clustered together on a series of short streets. In 1902 the provincial government built a one-room schoolhouse at the east end of the village. The original schoolroom had been a makeshift affair set up in the barn, in what had been the harness room. It was not until 1906 that Burnaby accepted responsibility for schooling in Barnet.

The North Pacific Lumber Company was at the height of its success when the mill was destroyed by fire on the night of May 5, 1909. A bigger and better mill—meaning one designed for greater efficiency and profit—was soon built.

When war broke out in 1914 so many skilled mill workers enlisted that the mill had to shut down. When it reopened after the war it was no longer owned by the MacLarens and Frank Ross, whose vision had put it on the map in the first place.

NORTH PACIFIC
LUMBER CO'S MILL
BARNET B.C.

The North Pacific Mill

The North Pacific Lumber Company's original mill was 300-by-50 feet, two storeys tall and built on heavy pilings. The pilings were encased in gravel and cement that was intended to make them "teredo-proof." The building was sheathed in corrugated galvanized iron. On its upper floor, logs became rough-cut timber, and on the lower floor the raw timber passed through the planing mill to become dressed lumber ready for the drying kiln. On the side of the mill property facing Burrard Inlet was a deck-cum-wharf 100 feet wide and 3,000 feet long.

28. Workmen's Quarters Store   Office and Mill   Barnet, B. C.

The Timber Deck

The timber deck of the original Barnet mill could handle logs that were up to 60 feet in length and 10 feet in diameter. Since there were 22 different saws that were raised and lowered by levers as needed, the men cutting the timber to size had to be both skilful and strong. While the new 1910 mill could handle logs up to 110 feet in length, the day of the automated mill was still a long way off.

The Company Town

As company towns go, Barnet wasn't all that bad. While the men in the mill worked a 10-hour day, 6 days a week without any such thing as overtime, by the standards of the day they and their families were well looked after. Their cottages were modern and well maintained and, most importantly, the children had a happy and safe environment in which to live.

The Post Office and General Store

Barnet's post office opened on January 1, 1900. The community's first postmaster, J.M. Poitras, also managed the general store, in which the post office had a corner. If at all possible, father and one or two of the older children would go by launch or on foot to Vancouver on a Saturday night to buy provisions for the next week at much lower prices than would be found in the company store. Where was mother? She was at home looking after the younger children, as usual! In many ways the company store was the "Forgetful Store," the place where one went to shop for those items that didn't get picked up in town.

Downtown Barnet
Barnet even had its own railway station. In spite of its modest proportions it was a scheduled stop for the CPR's *Agassiz Local.*

The Royal Mail
While the CPR's name trains could not be expected to stop at Barnet, through the use of a device that looked as though it had been invented by Rube Goldberg, the express trains were able to pick up mail as they sped through Barnet on their way to either Vancouver or Montreal.

A Great Place For Horses

James Barnet MacLaren was very fond of horses, and those employed at the North Pacific mill were very well cared for. The stable could accommodate 16 horses, and had a box stall for any that were unwell. A first-rate harness room was so well kept that it was used as the community's first schoolroom! The harness for each horse was hung on a wooden peg, above which the animal's name was printed. Teamsters were expected to get up at 5:30 to brush and harness their horses before going to breakfast. Their 10-hour shift began at 6:50 a.m.

Sikhs

A number of East Indian people worked in the North Pacific Mill. Most were over six feet tall and many were ex-British militia or policemen. Although they were invariably called "Hindoos," they were in fact Sikhs. They had their own quarters and did not eat in the company cookhouse, preferring to prepare their own meals.

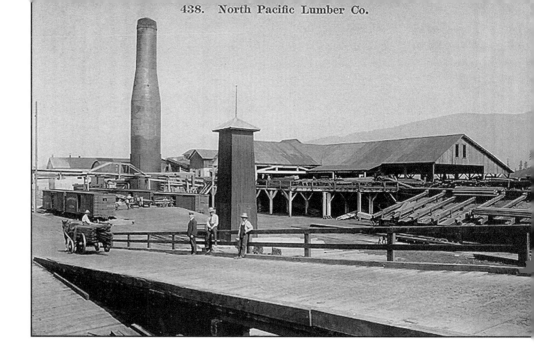

438. North Pacific Lumber Co.

The Fire of May 5 and 6, 1909
The fire that destroyed the Barnet sawmill began not long before midnight on May 5, 1909. It quickly engulfed the mill, and there was no hope of saving it. Two fire engines were sent out to Barnet on a flatcar from Vancouver, but they were only able to help contain the blaze. While the dry kilns and the piled lumber were saved, four CPR boxcars, as well as the mill itself, were destroyed. None of the workers' homes were in danger because of their distance from the mill.

Mills Burning at Barnet, B. C.
1:30 a.m. May 6th, 1909.

Ruins of Mill, Barnet, B. C.
Looking West, May 6th, 1909.

Vancouver

LET IT SNOW

Born and raised in Toronto, Philip Timms moved with his bride to Vancouver in 1898. Timms quickly became a great civic booster who delighted in the rapid growth of local industry, the activity associated with ships and shipping, the beauty of the city and its glorious natural setting and, above all, its mild coastal climate and relatively meagre snowfall.

But Timms did enjoy Vancouver's few weeks of snow each year: it happily reminded him of what he was escaping back east, where snow came not for weeks but for months!

Interestingly, even though the snowfall may have seemed more of a joke to Timms than anything else, the amount that fell on Vancouver in the years before the Great War was far more than we now experience during the average winter. From December 1909 through February 1910, there were 65 centimetres (26.24 inches), and from December 1911 through February 1912, some 62.2 centimetres (24.4 inches) of snow blanketed the city. By way of comparison, in the same winter months in 2004–2005, only 19.2 centimetres (7.83 inches) of snow fell on the city. While it may be hard for some to believe, back in the "good old days" of heavier snowfalls there were usually two or three weeks when it was safe to skate on Stanley Park's Lost Lagoon and Beaver Lake, and Trout Lake in east Vancouver.

In Timms' day the city owned little snow removal equipment. Vancouver's main streets were not all that well—or that frequently—plowed, and side streets were rarely, if ever, cleared of snow. Difficult as this made life for the drivers of both horsedrawn and motorized vehicles, it was just great as far as the kids were concerned. Schools often closed, and sleds were dragged up the hilliest streets to be ridden back down as fast as possible. Thick woolen clothes that sucked up water like blotting paper and the heavy wet snow that was unique to the coast didn't dampen any youngster's enthusiasm at all.

While the city's works department was ill-equipped for snow, B.C. Electric was well able to face winter's challenge, and generally could keep the streetcars running. The company had at least half a dozen non-motorized snowplows that could be coupled to the front of any piece of motorized rolling stock. As well, it had a number of cars that were powered sweepers. The actual brushes suspended below the powered cars looked for all the world like giant bottlebrushes. They would clean between the tracks as well as remove the snow from them. Finally, there were a pair of powered cars called flangers. They were able to clear not only the track upon which they were travelling, but the neighbouring track as well.

Timms, secure in the knowledge that it wouldn't last long, seemed to get a kick out of the snow, just like the kids. He took his pictures and produced his postcards from them. He then enjoyed labelling his winter scenes with captions, like "The Joy of the Easterner, "Our Two Days Winter" and "Must We Admit It?"

900. Our Two Days' Winter.
Winter, Vancouver, B. C.

Much Ado About Very Little

The snow lying on the tree branches at Hastings and Cambie suggests a fresh snowfall. On the right-hand side of the postcard the steps leading to the city's first permanent courthouse can be seen. From 1890 until it was demolished in 1911, the courthouse stood on what later became Victory Square.

The four-storey stone building across the street from the courthouse, built in the American Romanesque style, was the Flack Building. While much altered, it is still standing and hopefully can look forward to sensitive restoration. It was once a very good address for the city's barristers and solicitors. Note Timms' postcard caption.

A Winter's Sleep

This postcard shows Timms at his photographic best. It has everything: composition, contrast and a subject of almost universal appeal—ships. The wharf belonged to the Union Steamship Company. Among the ships huddled together, as though against the snow and winter winds, was the *Senator*.

Launched in 1880, the *Senator* was used by Union Steamship to provide a ferry service for Moodyville's mill workers. In 1894 North Vancouver municipality built a wharf west of Moodyville, at the foot of Lonsdale Avenue, to facilitate a scheduled service to and from Union Steamship's Carrall Street dock. The service lasted until 1900, when North Vancouver inaugurated its own ferry service.

901. Getting Home for Lunch.
Winter, Vancouver, B. C.

Getting Home for Lunch?

With the new Bank of Commerce on the right of the picture set to open on December 21, this 1908 postcard view of the intersection of Granville and Hastings pictures a line of streetcars at least a block long on Hastings. Captioned "Getting Home for Lunch," this postcard reminds us that at the time it was produced, the suburbs were only as far away as Mount Pleasant, Fairview and Kitsilano, and that many business people—particularly those living in the West End and Strathcona—would indeed have gone home for lunch. And while they didn't have email, iPods or cellphones, neither did they have to wait a half-hour or more for the next bus or trolley coach to take them home!

904. Must We Admit It?
Winter, Vancouver, B. C.

Snow on Granville Street

Timms pictured Granville Street between Dunsmuir and Pender in the winter of 1908–09. One wonders why there is an endlessly long lineup of streetcars at what does not appear to be rush hour. With its cars carrying signs on their cowcatchers advertising skating at Trout Lake and reminding everyone that the ice is kept swept, B.C. Electric obviously knew how to look after business.

Another of Philip Timms' Finest Cards

Seen here is the corner of Georgia and Granville in the snow—a view Timms entitled "The Joy of the Easterner." Timms loved to poke fun at those who had to put up with the vicissitudes of an Ontario winter. With the cutter in the foreground, the delivery wagons at the intersection and the CPR's Hotel Vancouver in the background, Timms' postcard has great appeal.

The hotel opened on May 16, 1867—just eight days before the first transcontinental train arrived from Montreal. The building was enlarged in 1894, and again in 1905. The 1905 addition, which can be seen to the right of Thomas Sorby's original "Châteauesque" creation was designed by Francis Rattenbury in the Italian Renaissance style. To be fair to Sorby, he was less than pleased with his building, which the CPR's penny-pinching forced him to build "without style." Rattenbury's creation was ultimately incorporated into the second Hotel Vancouver, which was built between 1913 and 1916 and is fondly remembered by many long-time Vancouverites.

Steveston

WHERE HISTORY ABOUNDS

A number of communities along the banks of the Fraser River bear the names of pioneer settlers—landings upriver like Port Hammond and Port Haney, and ports on the river's South Arm like Ladner and Steveston.

While Ladner is on the south bank of the Fraser's estuary, Steveston is on the river's north bank on the southwestern tip of Lulu Island, which was originally known simply as Island Number 1. It was not until 1863 that Colonel Richard Moody, commander of the Royal Engineers stationed at Sapperton, gave the island a more presupposing name.

It seems that the gallant colonel was accompanying Miss Lulu Sweet, an American actress who was travelling from Victoria to keep a theatrical engagement in New Westminster. As their ship passed along the southern shore of the large, flat island on their port side, Miss Sweet asked the name of the island. Ever the gentleman, Moody told her that since it as yet had no name, he would have it named "Lulu Island" in her honour. While history doesn't record Miss Sweet's reaction to the colonel's gesture, he was as good as his word, and in 1863 the name "Lulu Island" began to appear on government maps.

Even though approximately one-third of the acreage in the centre of the island is peat bog, as early as the 1870s the encircling lands, like those of the Fraser Valley, were already well regarded as ideal for agriculture and were available for homesteading. In 1859, to encourage settlement in both the valley and tidewater lands, Governor Douglas had the Royal Engineers survey the region. Following the survey, the Pre-emption Act of 1860 and its amendment of 1861 gave each adult male who was a British subject the right to homestead 160 acres in the mainland colony of British Columbia.

Moncton Street: Steveston's Finest

Steveston's townsite grew out of William Herbert Steves' crown-land grant of 1880. In 1888, by which time his land had been surveyed and he had town lots on the market, salmon fishing and canning had already overtaken farming as the principal reason for the community's existence. By 1890 Steves had already sold 100 lots. Approximately half the townsite was to be residential, while the other half would provide space for businesses and services. It was a unique community: by 1910—in the May-to-October fishing season—there was a population of Aboriginal, Japanese and Chinese residents that outnumbered their White neighbours by five to one.

Steveston's townsite centred on Moncton Street. Its business blocks were generally no more than two storeys, featuring elaborate false fronts that made them look much grander than they really were. The sole three-storey building on the town's main street was the London Hotel, which can be seen in the middle of the block on the right-hand side of Timms' photograph.

The London Hotel and its competitors all had bars and dining rooms that served both the travelling and the thirsty public. The story goes that in Steveston's heyday each of the hotels provided the first customer of the day with a free drink. Local tradition also tells us that there was even a bar on the river side of the dike to accommodate fishermen.

41

32. A Farmer's Residence.
Steveston, B. C.
September, 1908.

The London Brothers

Leaving Ontario for the West in 1877, Charles and William London chose to settle in what is now Steveston. They bought 200 acres, at $10 an acre, from Thomas McNeely at the south end of No. 2 Road. They not only farmed, but also built a modest wharf at what became known as London's Landing. Brother William built and managed a general store and a hotel at the landing. He also served as a Richmond councillor from 1883 until 1887. Unfortunately, he suffered from tuberculosis and was obliged to move to California to take advantage of its drier climate.

In the mid-1880s the federal government built a much more substantial wharf at London's Landing, where the sternwheeler *Transfer* could stop each day as it travelled between Ladner and New Westminster. A post office of sorts was opened at the landing in 1889, and was replaced by an official Steveston post office in 1890.

William's brother, Charles, was the farmer. He had dairy cattle, and successfully grew feed grain, fruit and vegetables. In 1888 he married Henrietta Dalziel and built the small house on the left in Timms' photograph. As the picture suggests, he was a rather successful famer. His much larger home, on the right in the photo, was built around 1906.

Steveston, B. C.

The Japanese Hospital

The Japanese Fishermen's Association, as part of its mandate to serve the Japanese community in Steveston, opened a small hospital in July 1896. It was established because, as the Japanese consul of the day said, "the Japanese [have] had to go to the white people's hospital [in Vancouver] where they experienced not only handicaps caused by lack of knowledge of the language, customs, etc., but also humiliating treatment." The hospital shared a building on No.1 Road at Chatham Street with the Methodist Mission to the Japanese and the Japanese School. In 1900, by which time the Association had become the Japanese Fishermen's Benevolent Society, $1,800 was raised to build the new 18-bed hospital pictured here. Each Japanese family, and those White families that wished to be eligible to use the hospital, paid an annual fee of $8. The fees covered the costs of operating the hospital. After the September 1942 internment of the Japanese, the facility was renamed Steveston Hospital. It was the only hospital on Lulu Island until Richmond General opened in 1966.

Sockeye Hotel

According to *Henderson's Directory*, Steveston's 1909 population was "500 whites and 2,700 orientals." While the directory listed all the White citizens, it made little effort to identify the community's Asian residents. It did, however, list "Chinese Firms"—12 in number. One was Mrs. Mary Lee's Sockeye Hotel. It had been built for Harry Lee, her American husband, in 1894. With its attractive second-storey boxed bay windows and a stylish pediment complete with dentil mouldings, the building had considerable eye appeal when Philip Timms photographed it in 1908.

The building has figured prominently in Steveston's history. During the fishermen's strike of July 1900, it was used as headquarters for soldiers of the Duke of Connaught's Own Rifles, who were brought from Vancouver to support the town's police chief, his sergeant and his one and only constable. In 1918, by which time the hotel had changed hands and become the Steveston Hotel, it was again used for emergency shelter. It was one of the few buildings to escape the fire of May 14, 1918, which destroyed much of the town, and was therefore able to provide refuge to many who had lost their homes. Its dining room served as Steveston's post office while the town was being rebuilt.

The hotel still stands on its original site on Third Avenue. It is listed in Richmond's Heritage Inventory as " … a two-storey, utilitarian structure with a flat unarticulated facade and a flat roof. It directly fronts the street without transition or landscaping." The hotel lost all its charm in a post-Second World War "rehabilitation," but as one of Steveston's few remaining 19th-century commercial buildings, it awaits (and deserves) restoration to its former glory.

Dredge "Beaver No. 2," in Steveston, B. C. 1908.

Ditches and Dikes

Much of Lulu Island is just six feet above sea level. In the days when Philip Timms was photographing Steveston, both winter high tides and spring runoffs that swelled the Fraser meant that the island could expect flooding to some degree every year. Richmond's first farms all fronted the river, and their owners were obliged to dike their lands at their own expense as best they could. To improve matters the municipality, created in 1879, began to build roads across the island, thereby encouraging farmers to buy properties that were some distance from the riverfront.

As a further encouragement to settlement, residents were permitted to cut ditches and grade roadways with the earth cut from the ditches. The municipality paid 10 cents for every cubic yard of earth graded into a roadway. By 1902 the municipality had ditched No. 2 Road across Lulu Island, and by 1885 had managed to complete the ditching and grading

of Steveston highway. Floodboxes were built at half-mile intervals along the dikes. Theoretically, floodbox gates opened at low tide, allowing the ditches to drain into the river or the sea, and at high tide they closed, thereby preventing seawater from flooding the land.

Roadside canals or ditches built by the municipality were from 8 to 10 feet wide at the top, and from 4 to 2 feet wide at their base. There were, of course, never-ending problems involved in keeping Lulu Island above sea level: ditches, especially where there were culverts, could become clogged; floodbox gates could fail to function; and dikes could be breached. Dikes failed more often than would be expected because colonies of muskrat made them their homes. Richmond had to offer a bounty of 10 cents per muskrat to help protect the dikes. Undoubtedly, many teenaged bounty hunters were ready and willing to protect the dikes!

The winter flood of 1905 was particularly devastating and affected Steveston severely. It was obviously time for a local diking commission to be established. Richmond created two districts, with Steveston coming under the authority of the West Lulu Island Dyking District Commission. In 1906 the Commission brought in a floating dredge, *Beaver No. 2*, to dig sand and gravel to be used in building a stronger system of dikes. This same self-propelled "steam shovel on a scow" did a great job, cutting a canal 33 feet wide along the shore to create an impressively substantial dike. Richmond's diking program of the day was financed through an assessment of $2.25 per acre, to be paid annually for 25 years.

In the years before the Great War, the provincial government was pleased to supply support in principle for Lulu Island's diking program, but absolutely no cash at all.

The Steveston Tram

In the early 1890s the CPR first considered creating a subsidiary company—the Vancouver and Lulu Island Electric Improvement Railway —to serve the communities on Lulu Island. Nothing came of the idea until 1902, when a light-rail line was actually built from Vancouver to Steveston. While the 16.6-mile-long line was well used by farmers to ship their produce to market, the canneries made little use of it. It was cheaper for them to ship directly by sea to their overseas markets than to move their cases of canned salmon to Europe via Vancouver. Even though the twice-daily passenger and freight service provided by the "Sockeye Limited" was popular with those travelling back and forth to the city, the operation failed to fit in with what would today be called the CPR's business plan. That being the case, the line was leased to the B.C. Electric Railway on January 20, 1905.

B.C. Electric quickly built a large substation at Marpole (Eburne) to power the line, which was electrified at a cost of $108,000. Weekday fares—Steveston to Vancouver and return—were 85 cents. Elementary schoolchildren travelled to and from school for free, clergy and high-school students rode half price, and all fares were lower on Sundays and holidays.

Attractive new interurban cars were built for the line in the company's New Westminster shops. The *Eburne, Steveston* and *Richmond*'s new trams, with their gold-trimmed jade green livery, were a sight to see. Passenger service was inaugurated on July 4, 1905, and continued until February 28, 1958.

B.C. Electric's Steveston line was the last to provide passenger service; the trams were replaced by buses. For B.C. Electric, the switch meant that its much ballyhooed changeover "from rails to rubber" was complete.

Gillnets

As the 20th century began, gillnetting was the approved method for catching Fraser River salmon. A gillnet is a piece of webbing with a mesh that catches fish by allowing them to pass through it as far as their gills, but no farther. Once caught, the fish have no way to free themselves, other than by breaking the net with brute force. Encirclement (seining) and entrapment (traps) were either discouraged or banned by early conservation regulations. Gillnetting was a particularly effective way to catch salmon at the mouth of the Fraser: its waters were muddy, particularly in June, July and August, making it difficult for the fish to see the nets as they swam toward them. Gillnetting was popular with fishermen not only because it was efficient, but also because it was labour-intensive, creating more jobs for them.

The gillnet was originally double-knotted and made of soft flax twine. Interestingly, flax has greater holding strength wet than it does when dry, and it also deteriorates less quickly in the water than does cotton. Originally gillnets were hand-knitted by local Aboriginal women. The average gillnet was approximately 900 feet long and 16.5 feet (60 meshes) deep. After 1885, machine-made lines gradually replaced the handmade ones. The factory-produced lines—mesh, lead line and cork line—generally cost between $120 and $150. Bluestone, in the tanks on the right-hand side of Timms' photograph, is copper sulphate in solution. It is used to dissolve algae from anything, including fish nets, immersed in it.

There is a reasonable possibility that gillnets were first used on the Fraser River in the 1830s by employees of the Hudson's Bay Company at Fort Langley. Many of the company's men were from the Scottish isles, where gillnets had been used for centuries. For the Japanese fisherman pictured here on the left side of the photo, mending nets was a never-ending job, as it was for all fishermen.

The Salmon Fishers

At the beginning of the 20th century, some 2,000 gillnetters were salmon fishing beyond the mouth of the Fraser River. The Fraser's fishing grounds stretched from Point Roberts in the south to Point Grey in the north, to a distance of five miles offshore. In season the boats were out at six in the morning and returned to Steveston at six in the evening, when another shift took their place to work until six the next morning.

The first boats used for commercial fishing on the Fraser were Native dugout canoes. It wasn't long, however, before flat-bottomed skiffs that were between 18 and 26 feet long all but replaced them. These skiffs were powered by oars and a sprit sail. Sprit sails were first used by the Dutch because they served well in shoal and tidal waters. A pup tent provided the only shelter. These Fraser River skiffs were gradually replaced by the much more seaworthy Columbia River skiffs.

Gas engines were first installed in fishing boats on the Fraser River in 1902. They were two-cycle Frisby and Hyannis engines. In 1918 four-cycle engines became popular. They cost between $150 and $200, and were built locally by the Easthope brothers.

34. Frazer River and Canneries.
Steveston, B. C.
September, 1908.

Garry Point

Lulu Island's southwestern extremity was named in 1827 by Aemilius Simpson, captain of the Hudson's Bay Company's schooner *Cadboro*, in honour of Nicholas Garry, who was deputy governor of the company from 1827 until 1835. Simpson was searching for a site that would be suitable for a Hudson's Bay outpost on the lower Fraser, and the *Cadboro* became the first ship ever to enter the Fraser. The place chosen was the historic site we now know as Fort Langley.

Early on, a large lantern was tied near the top of an old tree to guide vessels into Steveston's harbour. In time a jerry-built lighthouse replaced the lantern in the tree as the local guide to navigation. It was later dismantled, by which time the federal government had positioned a lightship at the mouth of the river. The Gulf of Georgia Cannery can be seen in the background of Timms' photo. Garry Point is now a beautifully maintained and quite delightful public park.

Vancouver

HASTINGS STREET

astings Street started life as the trail that meandered along the south shore of Burrard Inlet between Hastings townsite—the area along the waterfront north of today's Hastings Park—and Granville townsite to the west. Granville stretched along the waterfront between present-day Gore Avenue and Thurlow Street. Just to confuse matters, the famous Hastings Mill was located in Granville, or Gastown, as the village was popularly called. The centre of Gastown was Maple Tree Square, now the corner of Carrall and Water streets.

Hastings Street took its name from Hastings townsite, which was named after the honourable George Fowler Hastings (1814-1876). Hastings had been stationed in Esquimalt as commander-in-chief of the Pacific Squadron of the Royal Navy from 1866 until 1869.

While it might be difficult today to think of Hastings east of Richards as being a "good address," or a shopper's delight, in its heyday the whole of Hastings Street was a vibrant and prosperous avenue of stores and offices. Along with Granville Street, it was one of the city's two best shopping streets.

Its large department stores—Spencer's and Woodward's—and its other fine shops kept Hastings Street alive and well until after the Second World War. The fact that the interurban station was at Hastings and Carrall, and that many of the city's streetcar lines travelled along Hastings, at least from Main to either Richards or Granville, helped establish and maintain the street's commercial importance.

Sadly, most of the businesses have gone, and much of downtown East Hastings is now peopled largely by an army of individuals who, either through the abuse of drugs or because of mental illness, have a diminished ability to manage their own lives. It is, therefore, not enough today to plan and work for the rehabilitation of the many historic buildings along Hastings Street: the various levels of government, private agencies, the medical community and the police must make a serious effort to rehabilitate those who have literally come to call Hastings Street and its back alleys home.

Hastings and Granville

What may be Vancouver's most popular postcard view looks eastward across the corner of Hastings and Granville streets. Timms' photograph was produced sometime before 1908.

Perhaps the most interesting thing about the 600-block of West Hastings was the clock created for George Trorey by the E. Howard Company of Boston. Trorey, who had been a Vancouver jeweller and watchmaker since 1895, paid just under $2,000 for his new clock. It was first erected on the corner of Hastings and Granville in 1906, the same year in which Trorey sold his business—lock, stock and clock—to Henry Birks and Sons of Montreal. "Birks Clock" quickly became both a civic landmark and something of a trademark for the company.

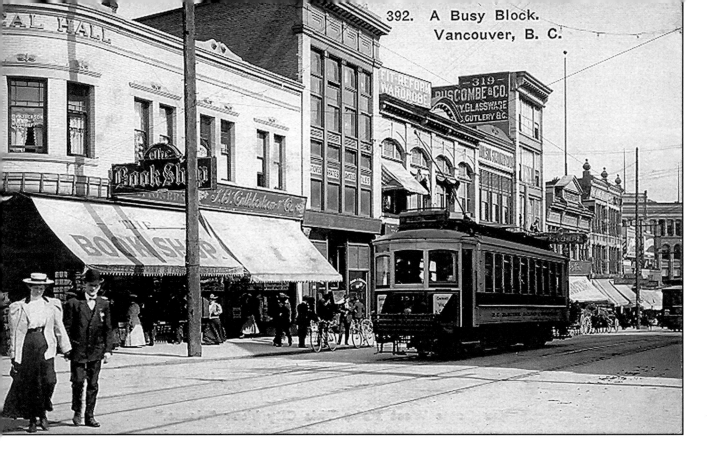

A Summer's Day

The awnings, bicycles and ladies' costumes suggest it was a warm summer's day when Philip Timms photographed the north side of the busy 200/300 block West Hastings in 1906 or 1907. This double block bounded by Cambie and Homer exists because Hamilton Street ends on the south side of Hastings. The block's attractive row of buildings featured a mix of two-storey shops in the late Victorian style and taller buildings in the Edwardian Commercial style. Important shops in the block included Woolworth's—popularly called the 15¢ store—and Buscombe's wholesale and retail china emporium. On the corner of Hastings and Homer stood the Book Shop, owned by G.S. Forsyth & Company.

Few of the buildings pictured have survived into the 21st century. In 1908 the Arcade, a popular "mall" of its day that stood at the eastern end of the double block, was torn down to make way for the 14-storey Dominion Trust Building, the tallest building in the British Empire at the time it opened in 1910. Interestingly, two prominent British Columbia photographers—Paul L. Okamura and Valient Vivian Vinson (King's Studios)—had premises in the 300-block West Hastings.

Shopping on Hastings

Philip Timms titled this postcard view of the north side of the 200/300 block "Shopping on Hastings Street"—a strange choice, in that no one in the picture is carrying a shopping bag or package of any sort! Still, it's a great picture of Hastings just west of Cambie on a fine summer's day. While the women stroll along in their seasonal skirts, shirtwaists and straw hats, the men all appear to be wearing warm, woolly three-piece suits. As a concession to the season, one or two of the chaps may be wearing Panama hats.

Not Your Average View

While this particular postcard view may not appeal
to a great many people, it will stir the hearts of train
buffs, particularly those with a special interest in
B.C. Electric. It pictures a group that includes freight
handlers, a train crew and a supervisor of some sort—
the fellow wearing the bowler. Standing off to the
right is a Chinese onlooker. The photo (attributed to
Timms) was taken on the south side of B.C. Electric's
first two-storey head office and interurban station (on
the left side of the photo). The facility opened on
September 2, 1898, and had been designed by none
other than Francis Rattenbury, the architect for the
provincial legislative buildings, which were built in
Victoria between 1893 and 1898. The original station,
with its offices above, was replaced in 1911–12 by
Somervell & Putnam's elegant building, which still
stands, even though it no longer serves as the
terminal for Canada's largest electric railway system
or as head office for the city's light, power, gas and
public transportation company.

The electric locomotive to the right of the picture
was one of serveral—probably 10—built in the
company's New Westminster shops between 1899
and 1909, the likely date of this unusual postcard. If
the locomotive looks like an octagonal wooden box
mounted on a wooden flatcar, that's because that is
exactly what it was. B.C. Electric did not acquire its
first steel purpose-built freight locomotives until 1909;
perhaps not surprisingly, they were British-built.

Vancouver, B. C.

The Woods Hotel

The former Woods Hotel, built directly across the street from B.C. Electric's interurban station, still stands on the southeast corner of Hastings and Carrall. Built in 1906, the Woods was designed by W.T. Whiteway, who was probably best known for his 1912 landmark World Building, now generally known as the Sun Tower.

The Woods advertised itself as a "hostelry [of] ninety large and beautifully furnished rooms, each one of which is provided with private telephone … light, heat, etc." The hotel also reported proudly that it had "more than twenty baths … elevator service [and] ten fire escape exits." The hotel's lobby featured "mission furniture, a tile floor, and art chandeliers."

Timms' 1908 postcard, picturing the busy intersection of Hastings and Carrall, places the Woods Hotel very much at the centre of things.

AST HASTINGS ST.
ANCOUVER. B.C.

TIMMS

Hastings and Gore

In the years before the Great War, Vancouver's business district extended eastward as far as Gore Avenue, beyond which lay the city's first residential neighbourhood. Developed because of its proximity to Hastings Mill, it was known simply as the East End until the 1950s, when the city's social planners took the name of the local elementary school—Strathcona—and applied it to the old neighbourhood.

Philip Timms' photograph looks westward along Hastings Street to Gore Avenue and beyond. Interesting buildings stood on each of the four corners of the intersection of Hastings and Gore. On the left of the picture part of the Empress Theatre can be seen. Standing on the southwest corner, it had opened on June 29, 1908, to provide "a regal home for drama." The theatre remained true to its purpose until it was torn down in 1940 to make way for a Safeway store.

The wagons stopped in the road were in front of First Presbyterian (later First United) Church, which stood across

from the theatre on the southeast corner. It was a well-designed frame structure that could seat 1,100 in its octagonal sanctuary. It was demolished in 1963 and replaced by First United's present building. Across the street on the northeast corner of Hastings and Gore stood the Salvation Army's Citadel and Hotel Welcome. Even though it was built in 1907, it was thoroughly Victorian, reflecting the prevailing belief that if a little decoration was good, more was better! Sadly, the old Citadel was replaced in 1949 by a much more functional but much less interesting Temple.

On the northwest corner of the intersection still stands the building seen in Timms' postcard—the Orange Hall. It opened with great fanfare in 1907 and was everything a fraternal order could want in a lodge hall. Designed by W.T. Whiteway, it was sold to the federal government in 1944 and redesigned into 27 suites to help ease the city's housing shortage. It has survived the years with considerable grace.

955. Hastings St., from Westminster Ave.   Vancouver, B. C.

Bookmark Postcards

Philip Timms produced this postcard as one of his series of bookmark postcards. The cards measure 6.375 by 2.25 inches and are rare. To date between 30 and 40 have come to light. That this particular bookmark postcard provides a view of Vancouver's old Public Library, the building that defines the corner of Hastings and Westminster Avenue (Main Street since 1910), may be a reflection of Timms' sense of humour.

In 1902 Andrew Carnegie had given the city $50,000 toward the cost of building a new library. It was designed by G.W. Grant, who went on to design the new City Hospital to be built in Fairview: it is now the Heather Pavilion of Vancouver General Hospital. The old library is now the Carnegie Centre, a community resource that serves some of Vancouver's least affluent citizens.

Just beyond the domed and pillared Beaux Arts library building, the Pantages Theatre can be seen. It is the oldest Pantages Theatre still standing in either Canada or the United States, having opened on January 6, 1908. It could be argued that the theatre is more than a national historic site: it is an international historic site. The building currently awaits sympathetic and appropriate restoration.

924. Inns of Court and Bank of Hamilton.
Vancouver, B. C.

A Good Address

Vancouver's first permanent courthouse was located on what is now Victory Square. Opened in 1890, it stood on the triangular piece of land until it was torn down, after being replaced in 1911 by the "new" courthouse on Georgia Street—now the city's art gallery. Not surprisingly, the city's lawyers wanted chambers near the courthouse, and those who could afford to do so rented space directly across the street in the Inns of Court, which stood on the corner of Hastings and Hamilton. It was at that corner that Lauchlan Hamilton began his survey that created most of the city's downtown streets and blocks.

Built in 1898, the Inns of Court was a Romanesque Revival brick structure highlighted by rough-cut stone ornamentation. One of its principal ornaments was an attractive turret topped by a well-proportioned conical roof that added a picturesque feature to an otherwise unassuming building. Given that the turret and its octagonal roof had obviously been removed by the time Timms took his picture of the building in 1909 or 1910, it can only be assumed that it was a very early victim of Vancouver's "leaky condo" syndrome! While a number of Vancouver's Victorian business blocks sported attractive turrets, towers and more than a little fanciful ornamentation when they were first built, many of the architectural embellishments soon disappeared: picturesque ornamentation, which was much better suited to a drier climate, just rotted away in Vancouver and soon had to be removed before more damage was done.

The ground floor of the Inns of Court was originally occupied by the Bank of Hamilton, which merged with the Canadian Bank of Commerce in 1929. As it happened, the building lasted longer than many of the city's other first-generation downtown commercial structures; it stood until 1952.

23. Bank, Telegraph and Ticket Offices
Vancouver, B. C.

Across the Street

On the south side of Hastings, two imposing bank buildings still stand like bookends propping up a rather nondescript collection of books. When Philip Timms took this picture around 1910, the "bookend" on the corner of Hastings and Richards was the Northern Crown Bank. It occupied a building designed by T.C. Sorby that was built for the Bank of British Columbia between 1889 and 1891. The Bank of British Columbia was created by a group of London financiers in 1862. When it opened its Vancouver branch in 1886, it became the city's first bona fide bank. It became part of the Canadian Bank of Canada in 1901.

At the other end of the 400-block, on the southwest corner of Hastings and Homer, stands the other "bookend" that in Timms' day was the local head office of the Royal Bank of Canada. Designed by Vancouver architects Dalton & Eveleigh and built in 1903, it was the city's first "temple bank." The neoclassical Royal Bank building has not suffered too greatly with the passage of time.

And what about the hodgepodge of "books" that make up the middle section of the block? When Timms was photographing Hastings Street, most of the buildings housed offices related in one way or another to the CPR. The railway's ticket office and its "telegraphic" office were in the block, as were the premises of both the Dominion Express and the Wells Fargo Express. The one building that had nothing to do with the railway or express services was a very small yet attractive building at 418 West Hastings. At the time when Timms took his picture, it served as head office for the Bank of Nova Scotia.

Hastings Street, West of Royal Bank.   VANCOUVER, B. C.

"Many Men Making Money"

The 400-block West Hastings still retains many of its original buildings, although a number of them are unrecognizable today, having been tarted up in the 1950s with modern false fronts. The tobacconist E.A. Morris (right side of photo, second from right) was at 435 West Hastings until the business closed. The shop had a most attractive Edwardian interior, with cabinets full of what seemed to be an endless selection of wonderfully aromatic tobaccos and cigars. In the centre of the store was a kind of "eternal flame" ready to be used by the city's gentlemen who couldn't wait to light up!

The banners, bunting and flags suggest that there was soon to be a parade in connection with some sort of civic celebration. The cost of the banners with slogans like "Many Men Making Money Means Much For Vancouver" and "In Nineteen Hundred and Ten Vancouver Will Have Ten Thousand Men" may well have been underwritten by the city's Progress Club, which had its own alliterative motto—"Promoting Provincial Prosperity."

Everyone Loves a Parade

The year is probably 1906, and a parade is moving eastward past the 500-block West Hastings. Nearing the intersection of Richards and Hastings is the Vancouver Fire Department's 75-foot Hayes aerial ladder truck. The city's first, it was bought in 1899 at a cost of $3,400 from the Waterous Engine Works Company of Brantford, Ontario.

As pictured, from right to left, the block included at number 501 the Bank of British North America. At 507 was the Standard Furniture Company and between 515 and 535 were the premises of David Spencer (Vancouver) Limited. At the west end of the block at 543 West Hastings stood the tall Molson's Bank. Not many years later David Spencer's business had expanded to the point where the company that bore his name owned and occupied every building in the block bounded by Hastings, Seymour, Water and Richards streets.

In 1926 the firm demolished the old buildings that stood on the eastern one-third of the block, and built what was intended to be the first part of the city's finest department store. Unfortunately, the Depression and the Second World War made further development of the block impossible. The Spencer family sold their business to the T. Eaton Company in 1948, and the rest, as they say, is history.

Vancouver

A WORLD-CLASS HARBOUR

Burrard Inlet, with its protected waters, 25 miles of shoreline suitable for wharfage, and 20 square miles of deep anchorage has to be one of the world's finest harbours. By 1910 an almost continuous row of docks and wharves ran along the south side of Vancouver's harbour from Denman Street in the west, to a point beyond Victoria Drive in the east. The Canadian Pacific, Grand Trunk Pacific, and the Great Northern railways had all built waterfront facilities. The CPR alone had Piers A and B plus a landing stage long enough to accommodate five berths. The Union Steamship Company had its docks, while the North Vancouver ferries had a slip next to a narrow wharf and floats that provided mooring for the West Vancouver ferries. Local entrepreneurs like R.W. Winch, Evans, Coleman & Evans, Hind Brothers, and Johnson Wharves had built facilities that could handle the largest freighters of the day—the ships of the Blue Funnel Line.

Shipping men at the time did, of course, have their dreams. They looked to the federal government to build a pier at least 800 feet long and over 250 feet wide, with 30 feet of water at low tide at the shore end. They also wanted warehouses, trackage and the necessary equipment to handle all kinds of merchandise. The anticipated completion of the Panama Canal and the increase in maritime trade that the new, shorter route to Europe was expected to bring added urgency to their appeal. Their dream was not to be fulfilled, however, until 1923, when the 1,200-foot-long Ballantyne Pier opened. Another dream of the early 20th century called for "the commercializing of Deadman's Island, a small tract of some ten acres lying just inside the First Narrows between [the CPR's] Pier A and the shoreline of Stanley Park." Fortunately, that dream was never fulfilled!

Like most Vancouver photographers, Philip Timms was drawn to the waterfront. He wasn't all that interested in producing photographic "ships' portraits": he much prefered picturing the people who sailed in the ships or worked along the waterfront. Consequently, his postcards have a liveliness to them that is often absent from the work of other commercial photographers of his time.

Australian Route, SS. Aorangi Entering Harbour.
Vancouver, B. C.

The *Aorangi (1)*

The Union Steamship Company of New Zealand (Union NZ) introduced its scheduled sailings between Sydney, Australia, and Vancouver in 1901. Between 1885 and 1900, the line had provided a regular service between Sydney and San Francisco. Restrictive American laws, however, forced the company to discontinue the run in 1900, and the service between Sydney and Vancouver was introduced to replace it. To make the run economically practical, Union NZ acquired a half interest in the Canadian-Australian Royal Mail Steam Ship Company, whose ships had been calling regularly at Vancouver since 1893.

The ship that inaugurated the new service was the *Aorangi (1)*, pictured here on Philip Timms' postcard. The Pacific crossing took 21 days; after leaving Sydney the ship called at Wellington, Suva, Honolulu and Victoria en route to Vancouver. The 4,163-ton *Aorangi (1)* made the trans-Pacific crossing regularly until 1909, when it was replaced by the new 8,075-ton *Makura*. The *Aorangi (1)* had an unusual career after being taken off the Sydney-Vancouver run. In August 1914 the ship was chartered by the Royal Australian Navy to act as a supply vessel. Manned by its civilian crew, the *Aorangi* took part in operations against Germany's Pacific colonies. In 1915 it passed to the British Admiralty and was sunk as a blockship at Scapa Flow naval base. Refloated in 1920, the *Aorangi (1)* returned to merchant service until it was scrapped in 1925.

Once a Sailing Ship

The coaling barge *Robert Kerr*, pictured by Philip Timms alongside the CPR's wharf, had a story to tell. In its earlier days it had been a barque. After a harrowing year-long voyage from Liverpool, England, it reached Vancouver in September, 1885. Since a marine survey showed the vessel to be no longer seaworthy, it was sold to William Soule, loading superintendent at Hastings Mill. It was riding at anchor in the harbour on June 13, 1886, the day of Vancouver's Great Fire, and more than 200 people took refuge aboard the ship, including its owner and his family. On October 3, 1888, the CPR bought the vessel from Soule for $7,000, and had it turned into a coal barge.

For 23 years the *Robert Kerr* was towed between Ladysmith (or Nanaimo) and Vancouver, carrying coal for the CPR's trans-Pacific liners and coastal steamers. The old hulk sank on March 4, 1911: it had been towed off course and dragged across a reef at the north end of Thetis Island. It went down with its load of 1,800 tons of coal intended for the waiting *Empress of India*.

A Busy Day On The Waterfront

Three ships are berthed alongside the CPR's landing stage in Timms' 1906 postcard, which he captioned "Along the Waterfront." This kind of crowding led the CPR to build its first pier—Pier A—in 1908. The new pier provided an additional 1,584 feet of berthing and sheds, enclosing 60,000 square feet of weathertight space for goods in transit. While it is not possible to identify all three vessels pictured, the ship in the foreground may be the CPR's *Monteagle*. Carrying both passengers and freight, the *Monteagle*, which was slightly larger than the *Empress of India,* the *Empress of China,* and the *Empress of Japan,* sailed with them to the Far East. Having a fourth ship on the trans-Pacific run made it possible for the CPR to offer a fortnightly service. Vancouver was the *Monteagle's* home port from 1906 until 1922.

After the Ball Was Over

The unidentified vessel docked alongside the CPR's wharf may have been the *Aorangi (1)*. Once all the passengers had said their goodbyes and were safely ashore, cargo had to be unloaded: a difficult, dirty, and sometimes dangerous job. One can only guess, but the crewman in Timms' picture appears to be operating the hoist used to unload the bales of wool being moved from the hold to the wharf. The chap on the far left of the postcard view may have been the tallyman, whose job it was to keep track of the number of bales being unloaded. Then again, he may have been just a guy killing time, who knows? Timms entitled this card "The Empire's Trade From Australia."

Stevedores at Work

Amid clouds of steam, stevedores are pictured unloading hemp from Australia. A lifting device, called a windlass and consisting of a horizontal cylinder on which cable or rope is wound, was powered by a small, steam-driven donkey engine that not only provided the power needed for hoisting the cargo from ship to shore, but in the process also produced the steam seen in Timms' postcard. The shrouds and ratlines—a spider's web of ropes— suggest that the longshoremen were unloading a sailing ship.

383 Struggling for Admission
Vancouver, B. C.

Struggling for Admission

Philip Timms' postcard pictures a shipload of would-be immigrants arriving in Vancouver from the Far East in 1905 or 1906. All appear to be male, and all are wearing their western Sunday best. The used postcard is dated August 14, 1907, and its message reads "Picture taken of transport with over 1,400 Japs on board ... [they] came from Hawaii. All are very well dressed." One can only guess at the nature of the welcome the newcomers received at the hands of Canadian Customs and Immigration staff.

The *Princess Victoria*

The CPR bought out the Canadian Pacific Navigation Company on January 12, 1901, and immediately became the dominant player in the coast steamship game. The first ship built for the CPR, which wanted to improve and expand the service of the old CP Navigation Company, was the *Princess Victoria*.

The vessel was built at Newcastle-upon-Tyne in 1902, and was ready for service in 1904. The ship was the last word in luxury and speed. Carrying a double crew, the *Princess Victoria* could make the trip from Victoria to Vancouver, then back to Victoria, on to Seattle and finally back to Victoria for refuelling—325 miles in all—within 24 hours! As Philip Timms' photograph clearly illustrates, the *Princess Victoria* was a coal burner.

In this image: 5 Our Lumber Industry Loading the Ships. Vancouver, B. C.

The Sailing Ships' Last Hurrah

In this Timms photograph, deep-sea lumber carriers are being loaded at the Hastings Mill wharf. Loading these ships was a slow and labour-intensive job. Dressed lumber was loaded through deck hatches, while lengthy timbers and spars were passed through stern loading ports. Once the hold was filled, still more lumber would have been stacked and secured on deck.

A Home Away From Home

Closely associated with the waterfront were the many hotels and taverns to be found along Water, Cordova, Powell, Alexandra and Carrall streets. They offered seamen, loggers, prospectors and cannery workers a home away from home with rooms, a barbershop, tavern, cafe and pool hall. One such hotel was the Rainier on the west side of the 300-block Carrall. Timms photographed the attractive brick hotel in 1910, not long after it opened.

And what's a seaport without sailors? In the foreground are a half-dozen seamen—two with duffle bags—making their way along Carrall, searching for such comfort as they can find in a foreign part.

THE PROVINCIAL EXHIBITION

On March 17, 1859, Colonel Richard Moody of the Royal Engineers wrote to Governor Douglas, letting him know that he had set aside "a very beautiful glen and adjoining land for the People's Park," and had already named it "Queen's Ravine." Moody rightly assumed that Douglas would approve. The park separated the military reserve at Sapperton from New Westminster, capital of the newly created crown colony of British Columbia. It wasn't long before "Queen's Ravine" became "Queen's Park." By 1868 land had been cleared to provide more than enough space in the park for a racetrack.

In 1889–90 the next major development in the park took place. It had been decided that the city's annual fair would no longer be held in an inadequate old building on Market Square, but in a special pavilion to be erected in Queen's Park. The exhibition building would be managed by the Royal Agricultural and Industrial Society of British Columbia, which had started life in 1867 as the New Westminster District Agricultural Society. Since its inception the society had sponsored an agricultural fair each fall, awarding prizes for superior livestock and farm produce. The new building at Queen's Park, designed by G.W. Grant, was ready in time for the 1890 fair, the first of a long series of annual shows known as the Provincial Exhibitions.

By 1905 New Westminster's Provincial Exhibition was recognized nationally as one of the country's significant fall fairs by being chosen to host the Canadian National Exhibition or "Dominion Fair," as it was popularly called. Federal funding of $50,000—a huge amount of money in 1905—was provided to help meet the costs involved in adding new buildings to house the much larger fair. While the Dominion Fair was judged to be a success, incessant rain cut attendance to the point where the event ended in the red financially.

In 1914 the Provincial Exhibitions were cancelled for the duration of the Great War. Initially the exhibition buildings became barracks for recruits posted to New Westminster. As the war dragged on, women of the Canadian Red Cross staffed Casualty Unit number 11 at Queen's Park.

A big celebration was planned for 1929 to mark the 60th anniversary of the founding of New Westminster's Provincial Exhibition. The special guest at this diamond jubilee celebration was to be the Right Honourable Winston Churchill. Things didn't work out as planned, however. At 6:00 a.m. on July 14, 1929, fire crews were called to Queen's Park, where the wooden exhibition buildings were on fire. It wasn't long before almost all the frame structures were in flames. The fire brigade could do no more than work to keep the conflagration from spreading to the nearby residential area. Within an hour and a half nearly all was destroyed: a few cattle sheds, a banquet hall and the old Fisheries Building were all that was left.

In spite of everything the fair was held as planned. A lot of makeshift arraignments had to be made, and for the most part exhibits and other

Spending Their Money

Spending Their Money

Fairs everywhere always had a midway of some sort, and New Westminster was no exception. Games of skill and games of chance, as well as "exotic dancers," freak shows, and gypsy fortune tellers all helped fair-goers part with their cash. Timms' bookmark postcard—a format that had some popularity in its day—pictured a few of the attractions that were helping draw a crowd. In the distance a large tent in which meals would have been served can be seen. At smaller stands strategically located throughout Queen's Park, tea and light refreshments would have been sold by the women of the Anglican, Methodist, Presbyterian and other churches to help raise funds for their particular congregations.

attractions were under canvas. Churchill's presence guaranteed a crowd of record size at the fair's opening.

As things turned out, the 1929 fair was New Westminster's last Provincial Exhibition. When the Queen's Park buildings burned, it was already becoming apparent that Vancouver's annual exhibition—first staged in 1910—was fast attracting more exhibitors and visitors than was New Westminster's fair. Declining revenue, the cost of rebuilding and the hardship imposed on so many by the Great Depression conspired to bring an end to New Westminster's annual Provincial Exhibition.

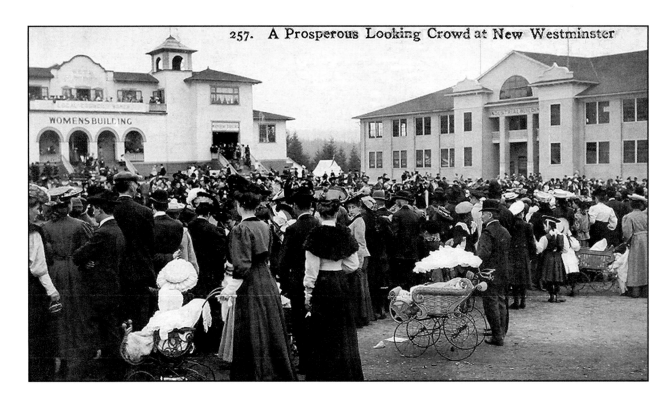

257. A Prosperous Looking Crowd at New Westminster

WOMENS BUILDING

The Crowd Gathers

Timms' postcard features a crowd listening to the opening day speeches at New Westminster's fair. The women's costumes suggest the picture dates from 1905 or 1906. The wicker prams and strollers are wonderful. Note the sunshade on the one being guarded by father—or is it grandfather?

The Art Show

In that Philip Timms was one of the original owners of Vancouver's Art Emporium, it is not surprising that he found the art exhibit at the 1906 Provincial Exhibition worth photographing. Six of the ten people viewing the display are children. Could this perhaps be a posed photograph?

A Bountiful Harvest

The work done by women of New Westminster and the Fraser Valley was recognized at each year's provincial fair. Chilliwack District's colourful and carefully arranged display appears to include jams, jellies and preserves—sure signs of women at work. Women were also much involved in picking the fruit, growing the vegetables and producing the butter pictured. With the erection of the Women's Building for the 1905 and succeeding exhibitions, women's contribution to the home, farm and community received increased, well-deserved recognition.

Panorama View of Fair Grounds.

New Westminster, B. C.

Queen's Park In 1905

The citizens of New Westminster were justly proud of their exhibition buildings in Queen's Park. Designed by G.W. Grant, the large building on the left in Timms' picture postcard was ready for the first fair, held in 1890. Grant was an architect of recognized stature, being the man who later designed Vancouver's Carnegie Library in 1900, the new Vancouver General Hospital (now the hospital's Heather Pavilion) in 1903, and other landmark structures in both Vancouver and New Westminster.

The Women's Building and the Industrial Building can also be seen beyond the racetrack. These and most of the other exhibition buildings were destroyed by fire on July 14, 1929. While the buildings were never replaced, the fire insurance payout the city received was used to cover the costs involved in building Queen's Park Arena. Originally intended to serve as a civic auditorium, over the years the arena has served chiefly as a home for ice hockey and box lacrosse.

Livestock on Parade
Beautiful Clydesdales were a surefire attraction at New Westminster's annual Provincial Exhibition. Timms' photographed three of these magnificent draft horses being judged in front of the main exhibition building. Which one got the blue ribbon we will never know.

Merry Christmas!

While a picture of a hefty prize bull being judged at one of New Westminster's annual exhibitions may have a certain appeal, Timms' overprint that allowed the postcard to be sold as a Christmas card seems a little bizarre. It's hard to imagine Edwardian matrons sending the card to their friends and relations but, as the saying goes, there's no accounting for taste.

MARCHING ALONG TOGETHER

One hundred years ago parades were much more important in people's lives than they are today. We have television with its VCRs and DVDs, the Internet and movies in all shapes and sizes. Our grandparents had none of these amenities in their homes to provide them with entertainment or amusement. They may have had a phonograph, or even a magic lantern, but that was about it. Many people entertained themselves by playing a musical instrument—most likely a piano or parlour organ—or by reading or playing cards. The men may have been involved in a lodge or, if relatively young, in a field sport, and the women would have had crafts like sewing and knitting that had a practical purpose justifying the time and attention devoted to them. And speaking of time, neither men nor women would have had that much time or money for "idle entertainment." But parades were free for everyone to enjoy!

In the Golden Age of Postcards, from 1900 to 1910, those who lived in larger Canadian centres like Vancouver could expect to see several parades in any given year. There would have been a parade on Empire Day (May 24), on Dominion Day (July 1) and, without fail, a Labour Day parade on the first Monday in September. In all likelihood there would also have been an Orangeman's parade on the "Glorious Twelfth" of July. And should any members of the British royal family—or any royal family for that matter—be in town, there was bound to be at least a military escort and band on hand to greet and accompany the visitors to their destination.

Then there was the circus! Whether the circus was large or small, there was always a parade from the Great Northern yards off Main Street to wherever it was that the circus was performing. One of the finest parades was staged by Barnum & Bailey on August 20, 1910, and among the army of photographers snapping pictures of it was Philip Timms. He would have loved the parade with its seven brass bands and a steam organ, or calliope.

Timms came from a family of musicians. His father, a printer by trade, was choirmaster and organist in at least two churches in Toronto. He was also Canada's first publisher of sheet music. Philip and his four brothers were all musical, first singing in boys' choirs, then functioning as organists and choirmasters in different Anglican parishes and other congregations. Playing several instruments, they were also members of the Mount Pleasant Band, and later the city's Citizens' Band. Philip Timms played both the piano and organ, as well as the French horn. At one point in his musical career, Timms' musical ideas weren't all that well received: he had tried to introduce violins and a trumpet into a congregation's services.

Regardless, Philip Timms' enthusiasm for parades, with all their colour and music, provided grist for his photographic mill. And for that we are thankful.

Mothers, Wives and Sweethearts.
Vancouver, B. C.

In the Heat of Summer

What can be said about a Timms' bookmark postcard entitled "Mothers, Wives and Sweethearts" that fails to tell us where or when the photo was taken? Not much, but certainly we can see that the troops were assembled on the Cambie Street Grounds, and the soldiers were men of the 6th Regiment, Duke of Connaught's Own Rifles. The buildings that can be seen on the north side of Dunsmuir Street were the YMCA on the left and the Vancouver Athletic Club on the right. The postcard probably dates from 1907 or 1908.

Boys Will Be Boys

For many years two old cannons stood on either side of the entrance to the Beatty Street Drill Hall. They were, of course, irresistible attractions for the young fry. The drill hall was built between 1899 and 1901 by the federal Department of Public Works. The building was in the Medieval style, which at the time was deemed most appropriate for military drill halls and armouries. The cannons have long since been replaced by a much less appealing pair of Second World War tanks.

389   Our First Line of Defence
Vancouver, B. C.

The "Kilties"

Pipers of the 72nd Seaforth Highlanders of Canada lead the troops from the Beatty Street Drill Hall. The regiment was allowed to use the name, "72nd Seaforth Highlanders" for the first time in 1910. The regiment went to France on August 18, 1916, and fought with distinction at Vimy Ridge, Ypres and the Somme.

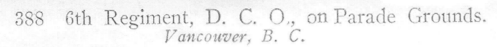

388 6th Regiment, D. C. O., on Parade Grounds.
Vancouver, B. C.

The DCOR

The 6th Regiment Duke of Connaught's Own Rifles (DCOR) is parading on the Cambie Street Grounds that occupied the block bounded by Cambie, Georgia, Beatty and Dunsmuir streets.

Dominion Day

These two Timms postcards picture the 1909 Dominion Day parade. Soldiers and sailors are seen making their way along Cordova Street toward Carrall. They were probably marching to the Cambie Street Grounds. The soldiers were men of the 6th Regiment Duke of Connaught's Own Rifles (DCOR), while the sailors were from a ship of the Royal Navy stationed at Esquimalt. The Canadian navy was not created until 1910.

The Duke of Connaught's Own

A military march past at Cambie Street Grounds always attracted a crowd. The troops on parade were men of the 6th Regiment DCOR. The regiment, with its white pith helmets, grew out of the Vancouver Battery of the B.C. Brigade of Garrison Artillery, formed in 1893.

In 1899 the Vancouver Battery was converted into the 6th Battalion Rifles, receiving the name 6th Regiment Duke of Connaught's Own Rifles on May 1, 1900, the Duke's birthday. After the Second World War it became an armoured (tank) regiment, and since 1958 it has been known as the B.C. Regiment (DCO). Prince Arthur, Duke of Connaught (1850–1942), was the third son of Queen Victoria and Prince Albert.

Tons and Tons of Elephants

Barnum & Bailey's Greatest Show on Earth gave two performances in Vancouver on Saturday, August 20, 1910. This Timms picture of the circus parade features some of the elephants. Probably many people lining Hastings Street had never before seen one elephant, let alone 40 of the beasts! The circus was huge—its people, including everyone from acrobats to zebra keepers, numbered 1,200 men and women. There were 700 horses and 100 cages of wild animals as well.

On Being First

Seen here in a carriage on the occasion of her 21st birthday is Edith Jackson. Edith was born in August 1886 and was later acclaimed Vancouver's first baby. Facing her, but unseen in the postcard, was Mayor Alexander Bethune. Others felt the title should have been theirs, but at the time Timms produced his postcard, Miss Jackson was regarded as the rightful claimant. To mark the occasion of her birthday, the mayor and aldermen presented her with a silver tea service and an illuminated address, signed by them all. Edith and the mayor paraded around the city and were warmly greeted by onlookers.

In the 1930s Major J.S. Matthews, by then Vancouver's city archivist, wasn't all that convinced that Edith Jackson was the rightful title holder. He doggedly conducted a lengthy search, and in 1939 found that someone named Margaret Mitchell had documented proof that she had been born in Vancouver on April 22, 1886, just 20 days after the city was incorporated. While Edith got the tea service, Margaret, who was living in the United States when Matthews caught up with her, belatedly got the title.

Britannia

THE EMPIRE'S LARGEST COPPER MINE

In 1859 George Richards, captain of HM Survey Ship *Plumper*, named the mountains on the east side of Howe Sound the Britannia Range, honouring a famous ship of the British navy. At the base of the mountains, Britannia Beach, 32 miles north of Vancouver, became the site of the British Empire's largest copper mine.

The ore deposits above Britannia Beach were discovered in 1888 by Dr. Alexander A. Forbes, who was employed by the federal government to look after the medical needs of Aboriginal people living around Howe Sound who had survived a severe smallpox epidemic that had decimated their population. Forbes lived on the west side of Howe Sound, and in his spare time enjoyed prospecting. He worked the same site above Britannia Beach off and on for 10 years.

In 1898 a trapper with the singularly appropriate name of Oliver Furry somehow discovered the location of Forbes' diggings. With the encouragement of a group of furriers, he staked out five claims in what became known as the Jane Basin, where Forbes had been working. The site is about three miles from tidewater. Ownership of the claims quickly passed from Furry to a Victoria fur wholesale firm, Boscowitz & Co. Boscowitz and his Vancouver agent, Thomas T. Turner, established a company and set up camp in the Basin, which is 3,500 feet above sea level. A four-mile trail ran between the camp and Britannia Beach. A small number of workmen were hired to dig a 132-foot-long tunnel and a few exploratory drifts, but they found nothing. Next on the scene were Joseph Adams and his friend Howard Walters of Libby, Montana. They were convinced that the mine had potential and in 1899 bought a seven-tenths' interest in the Boscowitz-Turner holdings for $35,000.

On January 16, 1901, the Vancouver *Province* reported that the Boscowitz property had "exposed an [ore] vein 26 feet wide ...." While the deposits proved to be mainly copper, there was also gold and silver to be found. It was not long before the Britannia Copper Syndicate Limited was formed to attract funding. While the syndicate ended up being financially controlled by New York interests, management remained local.

Things began to move more quickly in 1903, by which time the infusion of new capital allowed the mine to be expanded and service buildings to be built at Jane Basin. Dormitories and cottages were quickly built and it wasn't long before families were able to move to the mine site. Soon ore was being moved by aerial tramway to the newly built concentrator down at Britannia Beach. In 1905 the first concentrated ore was shipped to the company's smelter at Crofton on Vancouver Island.

In 1912 J.W.D. Moodie, a native of Hamilton, Ontario, who was involved in mine management in Utah, was made general manager and vice-president of the company by its New York owners. At the same time $5 million was made available to him to upgrade and modernize the operation at Britannia. By 1920 Moodie had been able to make Britannia, with its workforce of over 600 employees, one of the world's top copper producers. His life and time at Britannia were not without difficulty, though. Tragedy hit the Jane Camp on March 21, 1915, when an avalanche struck the community, killing more than 50 people and virtually destroying the townsite. Well away from Jane Basin a new and safer townsite—the Tunnel or Mount Sheer camp—was built.

The avalanche of 1915 was not the end of adversity. On March 7, 1921, Mill Number 2 burned to the ground. Built in 1913–1914, it was designed to take advantage of a newly patented flotation process that made the refining of low-grade ore economically practical. The second mill increased productivity from 200 to 2,000 tons of concentrate per day. On Sunday, October 28, 1921—just seven months after the mill burned—inordinately heavy rains caused Britannia Creek to overflow its banks. The Britannia Beach townsite quickly became no more than a mass of wreckage. Thirty-seven people were killed, and many more injured; the Beach community had to be completely rebuilt.

The new mill—Number 3—was an upscale version of the second mill, having been built of steel on a concrete foundation. The peak production year at Britannia was 1929, when the mill was producing 6,300 tons of ore per day. At that time the mines at Britannia were acknowledged to be the largest producers of copper in the British Empire.

By the late 1950s Britannia was facing difficulties that suggested the mine's productive life was coming to an end. The price of copper had fallen appreciably, open pit mines in the Interior and on Vancouver Island could extract ore more cheaply (and profitably) than Britannia, and the worldwide demand for copper had lessened. Although Britannia closed in 1958, it was purchased and its life extended until 1974 by the Anaconda Mining Company. In that year increased operating costs, taxation and growing competition from more efficient and productive mines brought about the permanent end to mining at Britannia.

Even though the mining ended, the townsite at Britannia Beach continues to be a viable community, having developed a life of its own. Since 1975 it has been the site of the British Columbia Museum of Mining.

Children at Play at Britannia Beach
Timms' photos of family life at Britannia, such as this one showing children on swings and a friendly dog, are exceptional. The washing on the clotheslines suggests it must have been a Monday washday.

Britannia Beach, B. C.

The Community's Lifeline

Like most other B.C. coastal communities, Britannia was accessible only by sea, until BC Rail completed its rail line along the eastern shore of Howe Sound between Horseshoe Bay and Squamish in 1956. The ship docked at Britannia Beach, Captain John Cates' Terminal Navigation Company's *Bowena,* would have provided a welcome contact with the outside world. When Philip Timms took this picture in the early 1900s, the *Bowena* stopped at Britannia at least twice a week. It was licensed to carry 500 passengers in winter and 2,000 in summer, and served Bowen Island and Squamish as well as Britannia. The Union Steamship Company bought out Terminal Navigation in 1920.

Britannia Beach Townsite

The concentrator on the hillside above Britannia Beach was an ever-present reminder of who and what it was that put bread on everyone's table: Britannia was a company town with all that implies. The houses had a certain sameness, with their board-and-batten siding and overhanging porches. The enterprising souls who lived in the cottage in the foreground obviously tried to add a little colour to their lives by planting flower beds. Even if the fencing was unlikely to keep the deer out of the garden, it would at least keep children and dogs from destroying the well-kept front yard.

At the Rock Face

It's doubtful that any miner sending this Timms' postcard to friends or relations would have said, "Having a wonderful time, wish you were here." Mining at Britannia, as at every other mine, was both dangerous and hard work. Rand machine drills were introduced in 1904–05 and, while increasing productivity, they didn't make life any easier for the men at the rock face: the new drills weighed over 100 pounds each and had to be carried on the miners' backs.

Gravity at Work

By 1912 the aerial tramway—used for moving ore from the mine head to Britannia Beach—had been replaced by a much more efficient conveyor "powered" by gravity. Being enclosed, it was an all-weather means for getting more ore to the concentrator in a day than the old aerial tramway could have moved in a week.

Be it Ever so Humble …

Life at the Jane Basin mine site must have been particularly difficult for families. Hard work was the order of the day for everyone. Drafty log cabins, wood stoves, no running water, and up to 40 feet of snow in winter must have made life difficult. When Britannia first opened, a walk from the mine to the townsite at the Beach and back was an eight-mile hike!

The Logging Camp

There was no shortage of timber at Britannia. The company's logging crew, pictured in front of what may have been their dining hall, provided all the timber needed. Logs would have been milled to size for pit props and other timbers needed in the mines, and to produce rough lumber for other company needs.

At the Beach

The mine workers' homes at Britannia Beach were very different from the more substantial log cabins at the mine head. The cottages at the Beach looked for all the world like the summer camps city vacationers might have built on Bowen Island or the Sunshine Coast. While such residences might have been attractive during the summer, they were probably cold beyond belief in the winter months.

STANLEY PARK

Ever since Stanley Park was officially opened on September 27, 1888, every camera-toting visitor has taken his or her full quota of pictures. For those visitors without cameras, there have always been dozens of different postcard views of the park available for purchase. In the Golden Age of Postcards (1900 through1910) there were at least 25 commercial photographers producing Stanley Park views. Those who collect old Vancouver postcards are tempted to believe that there isn't a single tree in the park that hasn't been photographed at least a dozen times!

Never one to miss a good thing, Philip Timms had a wide assortment of Stanley Park postcards for sale. As usual, his photographic cards are full of people doing all sorts of interesting things.

A Day in the Park
Relatively few Edwardians had cars, and in Vancouver, as in other cities, the principal means of transportation was the streetcar. Seen below are visitors making their way from the streetcar turnaround to Stanley Park by way of the bridge across the western end of Coal Harbour. The bridge was replaced in 1913 when landfill made it possible for a simple causeway to be built. Could it be that the lad leaning against the large tree is looking into the viewfinder of an early Kodak Brownie camera? The box camera was first introduced in February 1900, and sold for a dollar.

The Hollow Tree

Certainly the most photographed tree in Stanley Park is the Hollow Tree. Over the past century it has gone from being the Hollow Tree to being the hollow stump: winter storms and rot have reduced it to its present height and condition. Still, with a little imagination it is easy to picture the carriages, buggies and early automobiles stopping to be photographed at the tree in the years before the Great War.

Note the "brake," that is, the wooden rod attached to the collar of the horse on the right and to the buggy wheel. It would have been supplied by the photographer to keep the horses from moving while the picture was being taken.

"Automobiling"

Pictured here is the first rally of the Vancouver Automobile Club, held in Stanley Park on Labour Day, 1907. The club was formed on July 31, 1907, and had 25 members. Eleven club members entered the race, and five actually managed to complete the course.

Vancouver's first motorist was William Armstrong, who bought a Stanley Steamer in 1899. By 1904 there were 32 registered vehicles in British Columbia, and by 1907 their number had grown to 275.

Touring Car near
Brockton Point.
Vancouver, B. C.

Travelling in Style

Timms caught the spirit of the times in this picture entitled "Touring Car near Brockton Point." Identifying the make and model of the vehicle may keep car buffs busy for a time. While we don't know the name of the owner of the rather grand automobile, we can be sure that he was wealthy!

In the background the Brockton Point lighthouse keeper's home can be seen. The light first went into service in 1890; the present lighthouse was built in 1915.

Second Beach

Stanley Park's Second Beach has always had a unique appeal. It is family-oriented and, from its opening in 1904, has been free of the slightly honky-tonk atmosphere of English Bay (First Beach), which had a pier, roller rink, bandstand, boat rentals, fish and chip shops and so forth.

When Second Beach opened, all it had by way of amenities was a bathing shed for ladies. It got its first children's playground equipment—six swings—in 1907. While Ceperley playground (1924) and the saltwater pool (1932) very much altered the appearance of Second Beach, it has always managed to maintain its family orientation.

The Glorious Twelfth

While the year is uncertain, there can be no doubt that Timms took this picture on the "Glorious Twelfth." Every conscientious, able-bodied Orangeman would have wanted to take part in the July 12th celebrations commemorating the victory of the Protestant Prince William of Orange over the Roman Catholic King James II at the Battle of the Boyne in Ireland. The victory confirmed the succession of Protestant monarchs on the British throne. James II was allowed to escape to France, and the Prince of Orange became King William III.

The parade is moving along Stanley Park's ring road on its way to Brockton Point, where a picnic and games would have helped mark the day appropriately. Note the animal paddock on the right of the picture.

THE CARNEGIE FREE LIBRARY

It has been suggested that the history of Vancouver had its beginning when the first sawmill on the south shore of Burrard Inlet—Hastings Mill—was built at the north end of what is now Heatly Street. Since many of the men working at the mill lived in on-site quarters, its manager, James Raymuir, opened the New London Mechanics Institute, which was essentially a meeting room and library for mill employees. In March 1869 it was renamed the Hastings Literary Institute.

Following the fire of June 13, 1886, that destroyed the infant city, a reading room was opened over a hardware store at 144 West Cordova. It was known as the Vancouver Free Reading Room and Library. Thanks to the effort of Richard Alexander, Father Clinton of St. James Church and Francis Carter-Cotton, the 400 books that had been in the sawmill library became the nucleus of the city's new library. The space above the hardware store soon became inadequate and in 1894 the mayor and council made it possible for the Free Reading Room and Library to lease a 46-by-46-foot room in the new YMCA building at 151 West Hastings Street. As the 19th century came to an end, the need for still larger library premises again became urgent.

In 1900 Alfred Allayne-Jones, a Vancouver lawyer, wrote to the George R. Maxwell, MP, asking him to write to James Bertram in New York. Bertram was Andrew Carnegie's secretary, and had a particular responsibility to vet requests for grants for the construction of free libraries. Maxwell wrote to Bertram, who responded that the City of Vancouver would receive a grant of $50,000, provided the City was prepared to spend $5,000 a year maintaining the lending library. Maxwell wasted no time urging Mayor Townley to accept the offer, and on March 19, 1901, Vancouver's City Council voted to accept Andrew Carnegie's generous gift.

After considerable debate regarding an appropriate site for the new library, a plebiscite was held. Vancouver's voters had to choose between a site favoured primarily by those living in the new and affluent West End, and the vacant land at the corner of Hastings and Westminster Avenue (later Main Street). The vote was 746 to 407 for the Main and Hastings location. That was the last time a public building of consequence was built on the city's east side.

The plan for a three-storey building submitted by George W. Grant, a local architect of considerable skill and imagination, was chosen. The new library opened in November 1903.

The building served as the city's main branch from 1903 until 1957, when a new central library was built at Burrard and Robson. From 1957 until 1967, the museum that had shared the premises with the library used the whole building. After the Centennial Museum opened in 1967, the Carnegie Library building sat empty and decaying for a decade. Various uses for it were suggested, but City Council agreed that it should be remodelled for use as a community centre. The building was renovated, updated and ready to open its doors on January 20, 1980, as the Carnegie Community Centre. It continues to serve as such most successfully to this day.

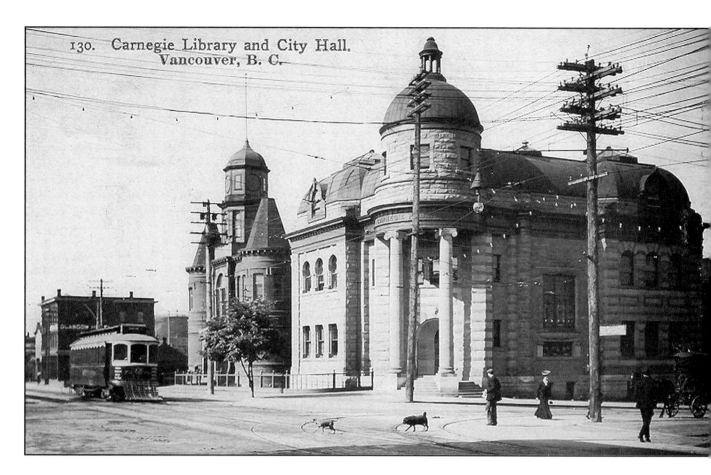

130. Carnegie Library and City Hall.
Vancouver, B. C.

9 Westminster Ave. Looking N.
Vancouver, B. C.

Edwardian Eclectic

Built in 1901–03 at a cost of $40,200, the Carnegie Library was designed by George W. Grant. The foundation is of Indian Arm granite, and it supports walls of brick faced with 10-inch-thick cut sandstone from Gabriola Island. With its neoclassical domed portico supported by a pair of Ionic pillars, its rusticated Romanesque stonework and round-arched windows, and its French mansard roof, the building can only be described as "Edwardian Eclectic."

Making the most of a limited and limiting site, Grant managed to create a handsome building. Timms' exterior photos are as good as they can be, given the presence of a forest of incredibly ugly power poles and lines.

Postcards for Sale

After the Golden Age of Postcards had ended, Philip Timms continued to produce postcards, but on a vastly reduced scale. One of his projects was creating sets of cards by special order for businesses, churches and other institutions—including the Carnegie Library, which he photographed in 1932. These cards would have been displayed and offered for sale in the library. The view seen here and others in the series reflect Timms' continuing commitment to quality.

The Fine Arts and Music Division

When the library first opened in November 1903, it was very well furnished: the Carnegie grant was large enough to cover not only the cost of the building, but also the cost of all necessary fittings, fixtures and furnishings. The building had hardwood floors, wood-panelled walls and eight fireplaces. In addition to the general reading room, there were special reading rooms for ladies and children, a chess room, a newspaper reading room, a picture gallery, a lecture hall, stacks and a circulation desk.

By the time Timms took this picture, the fireplace had become a magazine rack: one assumes central heating had won the day!

Stairs Anyone?

The old library's defining interior feature is its iron-and-marble circular staircase that continues upward to the building's top floor. It was designed and built by Bagster R. Seabrook, the general manager of Victoria's Albion Iron Works, at a cost of $2,279. The iron and steel used to build the staircase weighs 9,888 pounds. Its marble treads have been well worn by the thousands of people who have made their way up and down the stairs over the last 100 years. Unfortunately, a design flaw has given the stairs a decided list to the inside. All this small error in calculation means is that those who use the stairs are inclined to hang on to the lovely banister rather firmly.

The imposing stained-glass window that graces the stairwell was designed by N.T. Lyon and created by Robert McCausland Limited of Toronto. The firm is still in business, and it is doubtful that any city or significant town in Canada does not have at least one church with a McCausland window. The library's window naturally features literary greats: Shakespeare, Milton and Spencer. It was installed by Henry Bloomfield & Sons, a local firm that, like McCausland, specialized in quality art glass.

Eburne

THE NORTH ARM COMMUNITY

Eburne has a long history of habitation. Artifacts found in the 20th century in the Marpole Midden indicate that a large Aboriginal village stood on the north bank of the Fraser in the community that was to become Eburne and later Marpole. It is suggested that the site was abandoned over 1,000 years ago by the Native people because it was subject to frequent flooding. When the first White settlers pre-empted riverfront property in the 1860s, no signs of former habitation were seen anywhere.

In February, 1875, 19-year-old W.H. "Harry" Eburne arrived with his foster parents, the Cridlands, in what was popularly known as the North Arm—a community that straddled both the North and Middle arms of the Fraser River. Young Harry worked first for Fitzgerald McLeary and other farmers, then spent the winter cutting cordwood for logging outfits. He went on to pre-empt 160 acres just east of present-day Fraser Street, but soon abandoned the holding: the life of a pioneering farmer was not for him. In 1881 he opened a general store next door to the Methodist Church that stood near the foot of Hudson Street. The life of a merchant was much more to his liking, and he was soon a successful shopkeeper. He became the North Arm postmaster in 1885 when John Vermilyea gave up the job after only four months. Eburne continued to serve as postmaster until 1894.

The community was unusual from the beginning: it existed in three distinct places. Some of the inhabitants lived in what is now Marpole, others lived across the Fraser River's North Arm on Lulu Island, and still others, like Hugh McRoberts and J.W. Sexsmith, had their farms across the river's Middle Arm on Sea Island. At the time there were no bridges. Local visiting, therefore, often required a boat trip, as did the journey to the nearest market town, New Westminster.

It was only after Vancouver came into being in 1886 as the projected terminus for the CPR's transcontinental railroad, which was completed in 1887, that contact with the community on Burrard Inlet began to have meaning. The young city was soon seen as a relatively nearby and potentially lucrative market for the farm produce grown on Lulu and Sea islands, and for the canned salmon, lumber and shakes that were being produced in Eburne.

Back in 1885 the CPR had already set crews to cutting a road through the forest from what was to become Vancouver south to Eburne. Known as the North Arm Road, it eventually became Granville Street. Four years later, in 1889, two bridges were built by the San Francisco Bridge Company. The first crossed the North Arm, not far from Eburne's store, to Sea Island, and the second bridge crossed the Middle Arm of the Fraser from Sea Island to Lulu Island. Even though there were two bridges, they were always referred to as though they were one: first, the Eburne Bridge and later, the Marpole Bridge. (Also in 1889, the first Granville Street Bridge was built across False Creek.) Taken together, these bridges and the road through the forest that was to become Granville Street made life easier for those living in Eburne.

In 1892 Harry Eburne moved his store and post office to a point on the short stretch of road on Sea Island that ran between the two bridges. On October 1, 1892, what had been the North Arm Post Office officially became the Eburne Post Office.

Life got even better in 1902 when the CPR built a train bridge across the North Arm just to the west of the present-day Oak Street Bridge, and ran a line from downtown Vancouver through to Steveston. The train, which made two round trips daily, was popularly known as the "Sockeye Limited." In 1905 the trackage, officially designated the "Vancouver & Steveston Railway," was leased to the B.C. Electric Railway, which electrified the line and put three new interurbans—named *Richmond, Steveston* and *Eburne*—on the run.

In 1916 the part of Eburne running along the North Bank of the Fraser was renamed "Marpole," honouring Richard Marpole, the man who was the CPR's western district superintendent from 1897 to 1907. Among other things, he planned the development of Shaughnessy Heights and became its first resident. As it happened, by 1916 Marpole and Eburne had little in common. Marpole was becoming heavily industrialized with lumber mills and yards, while the portions of Eburne located on Sea Island and Lulu Island were principally focused on dairy farming and seasonal fish canning.

The building of the Oak Street Bridge in 1957 and the Arthur Laing Bridge in 1976 not only changed the face of Richmond—some say for the better—but also made Eburne and old Marpole into little more than place names from the past.

A View From the Bridge

When Timms took this picture he would have been standing on the Sea Island–Lulu Island section of the Eburne—later Marpole—Bridge. The view looks across Sea Island to the portion of the bridge joining Sea Island to what became Marpole in 1916. The distant ridge would be Vancouver's 49th Avenue.

A Sea Island Scene

The horse and buggy has just crossed the portion of the North Arm Bridge that joined what is now Marpole to Sea Island. On the left can be seen Harry Eburne's General Store and Post Office. The road pictured here led on to the second bridge that crossed the Fraser's Middle Arm to Lulu Island.

10. The Road to the Crops.   Eburne, B. C.

The Shingle Bolt Men

In these Eburne photographs Philip Timms has captured the spirit of the simpler time and more peaceful place they portray. Having said these things, we must not sentimentalize the scenes of Eburne as it looked in the opening decade of the 20th century.

Timms' own title for the picture at the top of the page was, "The Shingle Bolt Man." Doubtless the farmer in each of the pictures could have had any number of titles— dairyman, orchardist, truck gardener and so forth. To eke out a living, early settlers had to turn their hands to many tasks, including cutting cedar shingle bolts, which they could sell to one of the five or six Eburne shingle mills.

While the mills were in what is now Marpole, these two "shingle bolt men" would have been taking their bolts to a mill from their Sea Island or Lulu Island woodlots. And a long slow trip it was, too.

25. A Country Road Eburne, B. C.

Eburne Methodist Church

Designed by B.D. Poice and built by volunteer labour, Eburne's first Methodist Church opened in 1891. It stood on the corner of Cambie and River roads, directly across the Middle Arm from the Presbyterian Church. It had outdoor privies, a woodshed and a stable that was turned into a church hall in 1931.

When the Methodists, many Presbyterians and a few Congregationalists formed the United Church of Canada in 1925, the old church building, which by then was known as Lulu Island Methodist, became Richmond United Church. It relocated in 1960 to a site west of Cambie when the municipality wanted the old site in order to realign the railway that passed through Brighouse. The old church was boarded up and its fate was uncertain until 1968, when it was moved to Minoru Park, where it functions as a popular wedding chapel open to people of all faiths.

The building is a typical 19th-century Methodist meeting house, designed primarily for preaching the Word, congregational singing and to look vaguely ecclesiastical. The building reflects the Methodist preference for a style that could be called Romanesque Revival. The preservation of the old church was a remarkable achievement on the part of those who saved it from certain destruction.

35. Eburne Methodist Church, Eburne, B. C.

Presbyterians with a French Flair

Eburne's (and Richmond's) first Presbyterian church was located on the eastern bank of the Middle Arm, which separates Sea Island from Lulu Island. It was built in New Westminster at a cost of $1,665 and floated downriver to its site, which was near Millar Road facing the Middle Arm. The congregation had 26 members when its first service was held on July 4, 1886. The officiant was the Reverend T.G. Thompson, who concurrently served the first Presbyterian congregation in the new city of Vancouver.

Perhaps their Scottish origins led Sea Island's Presbyterians to build a church like one they would have known back home—one with French Gothic detailing in the windows and doors; a flèche, or slender tower, atop the ridge of the church roof; and, of all things, a cross atop the spire.

The interior of the church had no room for either Anglican or Roman Catholic architectural distractions, however. The "beauty of holiness" was not for the Calvinists.

Unfortunately, what appears to have been a particularly charming building was destroyed by fire on May 10, 1933. It had stood unused for a number of years when a careless neighbour, who was clearing blackberry brambles, set the building ablaze, and that was the sad end of it.

20. Richmond Presbyterian Church. Eburne, B. C.

The Town Hall

Richmond's first town hall was built in 1880 on a lot that was part of a five-acre plot sold to the township for $400 by Sam Brighouse. The parts of Eburne that were on Sea Island and Lulu Island were in fact parts of the new township created in 1879. The town hall was destroyed by fire in 1912.

That Timms captioned this postcard "We are at the Fair, Eburne, B.C." suggests that the building was pressed into service at fair time. It may have been used to display needlework, baking, preserves and crafts produced by the women of the community.

The Agricultural Fair

On a number of occasions, the Richmond Agricultural and Industrial Society attempted to sponsor a fall fair. While the fairs were well organized and attracted a reasonable level of interest and support, they were not all that successful. Richmond farmers seemed more eager to compete in both New Westminster's and Victoria's provincial fairs and in Vancouver's exhibition, where they repeatedly took top prizes in a number of categories.

38. Judging the Horses, the Fair.   Eburne, B. C.

A Rural School

Eburne's school was the typical one-room schoolhouse of its day. Until it opened in 1891, classes were held in Richmond's town hall. Built by the North Arm School District, the new building stood next door to the Methodist Church—now the relocated Minoru Chapel—on Number 2 Road near Cambie. The school appears to have had separate entrances and cloakrooms for boys and girls.

49. Our "Sun Flowers" at School. Eburne, B. C.

A Spacious Classroom

Eburne's one-room school was spacious, clean and bright. At the front of the room behind the teacher's desk was a blackboard, a map of Canada and a world globe. Since the teacher had nearly 30 children from ages 6 to 14 in her school, her job was not an easy one. The sole source of heating, a wood stove, was near the back of the room. It can be assumed that in winter the teacher and those who sat in the front rows didn't always get to enjoy its comfort.

51. Our School Room. Eburne, B. C.

Play Time

In 1910—long before the days of manicured, supervised neighbourhood playgrounds for children—the Fraser River's north bank must have been an enticing natural adventure playground. And it wouldn't be long before one of the interurban trains that ran daily between downtown Vancouver and Steveston would clatter its way across the 1902 trestle in the background.

Eburne, B. C.

THE CITY'S FINEST STREET

In the salad days of the picture postcard, from 1900 to 1910, Philip Timms' photographs provided a record of a street that lent, it has been said, a facade of sophistication to the western-frontier boom town that was Vancouver. That street was Granville Street.

Local shopping malls began to flourish after the Second World War; before then, "going shopping" meant a trip downtown. And for most people that trip was by streetcar. Shoppers could alight at Granville and Georgia—the Hudson's Bay corner—and make their way north along Granville to Hastings, then east on Hastings to Abbott, where Woodward's department store competed successfully with both Hudson's Bay and David Spencer Limited. Spencer's department store was on Hastings, about halfway between its two competitors. Shoppers could, of course, reverse their route, riding to Hastings and Abbott, where they would leave the streetcar, make their way along Hastings, then Granville, to Georgia, where they would get the "car" home. Either way there was great window shopping. For many women the trip downtown was a welcome mini-holiday from housework, and all for only 14¢, the price of two streetcar tickets.

While there were a number of good stores on Hastings Street, the best shops were to be found on Granville Street, thanks to the CPR. Why the CPR? Because the railway company worked very hard to develop Granville Street as the city's primary north-south axis, and its retail mecca. To that end it did all it could to make the four blocks between Cordova, where its imposing station stood, and Georgia, where its Hotel Vancouver marked the top of the rise from the waterfront, as appealing as possible. Substantial business blocks were built along Granville for Lord Strathcona, Lord Mount Stephens, Sir William Van Horne and Harry Abbott, all of whom had ties to the CPR. Three of these buildings, which had attractive ground-floor shops, were designed by New Yorker Bruce Price, one of the top architects of his day. His work for the CPR included the Château Frontenac in Quebec City and Windsor Station in Montreal. Both the Hudson's Bay Company and the Bank of Montreal, controlled by the same men who controlled the CPR, also saw fit to build on Granville Street. After Birks Jewellers, another Montreal firm, had relocated its Vancouver showrooms to the ground floor of its new office tower at Granville and Georgia in 1913, Granville Street had indisputedly become the city's premier retail and business address.

Granville Street's pre-eminence lasted for nearly three-quarters of a century, that is, until it was "malled" to death by the Pacific Centre, built in the 1970s. The huge, windowless mall that stretches over two blocks along the west side of Granville Street successfully drove the remaining businesses on Granville north of Georgia out of business. Only now, as the 21st century begins, is downtown Granville Street re-emerging as a "good address" for upscale retailers. Much of the credit for revitalization must go to the city's planning department, which has worked so hard to redevelop and rejuvenate downtown Vancouver.

103. Hotel Vancouver.

VANCOUVER, B. C.

The First Hotel Vancouver

As pictured by Timms, the CPR's first Hotel Vancouver stood on the southwest corner of Granville and Georgia streets. The simple gable-roofed structure was ready to receive its first guests on May 16, 1887—in time for the arrival of the first transcontinental passenger train a week later on May 23. Architecturally, the building pleased no one. Thomas Sorby, its architect, complained that the railway's penny-pinching forced him to create what he called "a building without architecture." One of the local papers described it as looking like "an exceedingly ugly workhouse." Matters didn't get much better in 1893 when a five-storey addition facing onto Granville Street was built. The effect was reported to have caused a local viewer to say that it "reminded one of a farmer who had married an aristocratic wife."

In 1900 the CPR announced that it would be razing Sorby's hotel and replacing it with a much larger one. Francis Rattenbury, designer of the legislative buildings in Victoria, was chosen as architect for the new hotel. He first created plans for a building in the Château style, but was told to rework the design in Italian Renaissance. Only the 80-room west wing of Rattenbury's hotel was ever built. He had a falling out with the CPR, and the second hotel, which incorporated his west wing, was eventually designed by Francis Swales. It opened in July 1916. As an historical footnote, it should be pointed out that Rattenbury's earlier effort in the Château style wasn't a complete waste of time: he resurrected and revised his plans to produce the Empress Hotel in Victoria.

113

The Hudson's Bay Company

The Hudson's Bay Company opened its first Vancouver store on Cordova Street, where it sold groceries, liquor and provisions to loggers, miners and fishermen. In 1890 the firm opened a branch store in the middle of the 400-block Granville Street. The company's next project was a new store on the corner of Granville and Georgia streets: it was the largest building on the block.

Timms' postcard pictures the Granville Street Hudson's Bay store as it appeared in 1906—enlarged, and providing space for 18 retail departments staffed by 150 men and women. The red-brick store was torn down in the mid-1920s and replaced by the second part of the present store. The third part of today's store, which faces onto Seymour Street, was not built until after the Second World War.

Granville Street North.
Vancouver, B. C.

Early Tourists

With or without his permission, a number of other publishers printed versions of this Philip Timms photo postcard. The Vancouver Tourist Association at 439 Granville Street first opened for business on June 27, 1902. Its banner tells the public that it is the "Headquarters for Visitors & Tourists" and operates a "Free Information Bureau." Tally-Hos regularly picked up sightseers in front of the Tourist Bureau, taking them to Stanley Park. Note the plank sidewalk.

A Little Bit of Glasgow

Built in 1892–1893, the main branch of the Bank of Montreal stood on the northeast corner of Granville and Dunsmuir streets for 80 years. Designed by Montreal's Taylor and Gordon, the wonderfully exuberant structure was in the Scottish Baronial style. While its design made it unique in Vancouver, it had many close relations along St. Vincent and other streets in Glasgow. Not surprisingly, its lead architect was a Scotsman, Sir Andrew Thomas Taylor, who, together with his partner, William Hamilton Gordon, designed many branch offices for the Bank of Montreal. Sadly, the building was torn down in 1973.

Looking North on Granville

One of the things that make Philip Timms' photographs so appealing is that more often than not, they are peopled. Many postcards produced during the Golden Age of Postcards look as though their photographers got up at 5:00 a.m. on a Sunday so their shots would not be spoiled by either vehicular or foot traffic.

While Timms' Granville Street postcard has lots of people in it, road traffic seems limited to just one buggy making its way up the street. The banner across Granville may be saying "In Nineteen Hundred and Ten Vancouver Will Have 10,000 Men." The Progress Club—a forerunner of the Board of Trade—was heavily into slogans that proclaimed the future greatness of Vancouver.

Post Office Corner

Vancouver's first purpose-built post office opened in 1892 on the southwest corner of Granville and Pender streets. It was the architectural creation of Thomas Fuller, the federal government's chief architect. Construction was supervised by a local architect, C.O. Wickenden, who had developed the plans for Christ Church Cathedral. During his 15 years in office, Fuller designed over 140 federal buildings in cities all across Canada.

After the new post office at Granville and Hastings opened in 1910, the old building housed a number of different government offices until 1925, when it was sold. Attractive though it was, it was demolished in 1926.

26. Where the Nations Meet
Vancouver, B. C.

Granville and Hastings

The western dress of the Sikh gentlemen crossing the intersection at Granville and Hastings says something about the pervasiveness of British education in India—and in British Columbia. Note the rolled umbrella. When Timms took this picture, any garb other than British dress would have been unthinkable on the streets of Vancouver.

The 1897–1898 MacKinnon Building, in the background of this scene, was considered Vancouver's finest office building when it opened. The Richardson Romanesque structure, with its rough-cut stonework and its rounded arches, was designed by William T. Dalton. Dalton was a keen alpinist and a member of the first party to scale Mount Garibaldi.

Port Moody

GREAT EXPECTATIONS

Port Moody is located at the head of Burrard Inlet. While most people associate the community with the coming of the railroad in the 1880s, its non-Aboriginal history actually goes back to 1860. In that year Captain Henry Richards surveyed Burrard Inlet and named its southeastern shore Port Moody in honour of the Royal Engineers' Colonel R.C. Moody. In 1859 Moody had built the North Road, thereby providing New Westminster with direct access to Burrard Inlet. The road provided the colonial capital with a "back door," should the Americans decide to move northward beyond the 49th parallel as they fulfilled their "manifest destiny." In the late 1860s Governor Seymour had the rough military road improved so that it could be used by wagons and sleighs. In 1874 a seaside resort popular with New Westminster residents developed at the Burrard Inlet end of the North Road; it had a hotel, cottages and general store. As well, by 1870 there were small, simple handlogging operations in business at the head of the Inlet.

On October 4, 1879, it was announced in Ottawa that Port Moody would be the western terminus of the transcontinental railroad. In no time at all the land along the waterfront east of the North Road community was in the hands of speculative absentee landlords. Their number included a future premier, a senator and a couple of judges! Lots were surveyed and in 1883 were selling at prices ranging from $1,500 down to $250. Prime property, as would be expected, sold for much more. Port Moody quickly became a typical boom town.

In 1882 the citizens of Port Moody petitioned the provincial government for an improved road. Victoria agreed to pay $4,500 if New Westminster and Port Moody would contribute $1,500. The money not only made improvements to the North Road possible, but covered the cost of the Clarke cut-off, which led directly into Port Moody. While the cut-off was originally little more than a trail, it did allow Port Moody to be reached without the need for a ferry ride between the end of the North Road and the town itself.

Life was good in Port Moody: the population was growing, there was full employment, and plenty of hope for the future. Only one small cloud was on the horizon, though no one paid much attention to it. On July 19, 1884, the local *Gazette* reported that the CPR was planning to continue its line through to English Bay. In August 1884 the CPR's general manager, William Van Horne, visited Port Moody on an inspection tour. He would not, however, speculate as to whether or not the railroad might be extended to Coal Harbour or English Bay, even though he had already talked with government officials in Victoria regarding both the need to build to the deep-water harbour some 11 miles west of Port Moody and the need for financial assistance in the form of land grants that would quickly produce much-needed revenue. The survey for the extension began in December 1884 and by June 1885, the right-of-way was cleared and ready for track-laying. In spite of both moral and legal protests, there was nothing Port Moody could do to stop the CPR from extending its line to Granville, soon to be renamed Vancouver.

The first through train left Montreal on June 28, 1886. After a journey that took five days and 19 hours, it arrived in Port Moody on July 4, 1886. But Port Moody's days of celebration were soon over. On May 23, 1887, after a brief stop in Port Moody, the first transcontinental train to do so continued on to be welcomed in Vancouver, Canada's new "Gateway to the Pacific."

Fortunately, many of Port Moody's citizens had come to love their community and were prepared to continue calling it home. Still, after 1885 Port Moody did go into decline, and by 1893 had a population of only 150. The village could only boast of a railway station with its telegraph and express offices, two hotels, a general store, two churches and a public school. It wasn't long, however, before the community's future began to look brighter: large new lumber mills like Canadian Pacific Lumber and J.R. Emerson were coming into production. Other, smaller mills also helped increase the number of available jobs. By 1906 Canadian Pacific Lumber alone employed over 200 men.

By 1910 Port Moody had three hotels, two new general stores, a branch of the Royal Bank, two doctors, a telephone office, P. Burns & Co.

Butcher Store, a Chinese laundry, a blacksmith shop, an ironmonger, brickyards and a boat builder. There were also 150 Chinese people living on the outskirts of the town in their own community.

The CPR was still very much at the centre of life in Port Moody, even though it had picked up its skirts and flounced off to the younger and much more promising city of Vancouver. Rail traffic, both coming and going, continued to increase.

The town had further cause for optimism in that real estate values were gradually moving upward. Whereas waterfront property had been selling at $20 a front foot in 1903, by 1908 it was again selling at $200 per front foot and more. But getting to and from Port Moody still wasn't all that easy. Roads were no ride in the park. The four-mile Clarke/North Road was in bad shape, and the Barnet Road was little more than a trail. Repeated attempts to have B.C. Electric extend its tramline from Sapperton to Port Moody—only four miles— never did meet with success. Most trips to Vancouver were made aboard the *Delta*, a steamer that brought workers from Vancouver in the early morning, then returned to Vancouver with prospective shoppers. In the afternoon it returned the shoppers to Port Moody and then transported home the workers who lived in Vancouver.

While Port Moody's great expectations may not have been met, the town did manage not only to survive, but grow larger. It was incorporated as a city on March 31, 1913, and continued to increase in population from that day forward.

10. The Old Station, Port Moody,. B. C.

Port Moody's First Train Station

By the time Philip Timms took this photograph of the CPR's first Port Moody station in 1907, it was looking a little the worse for wear. Built in 1885, it stood nearly a mile west of the centre of town, along an unimproved and poorly lit road. The location was chosen because it was adjacent to a site that provided good moorage for the ships that would be travelling to and from the Far East, earning much-needed revenue for the railway. The two-storey station was built by the San Francisco Bridge Company. With its attractive gambrel roof, dormers and whimsical Victorian trim, the structure had its own special appeal.

In 1907 the CPR built a new station to one of its standardized floor plans: Number Nine in the railway's design book. The second station was a half mile closer to town and, when it opened, the old station became the office for Port Moody's first oil refinery.

Places to Stay

In 1910 Port Moody had three hotels and three boarding houses. Two of the boarding houses—Mr. Ingalls' and Mrs. Ennis'—were for White residents, while Gin No's boarding house was for Chinese workers. Pictured is Oliver Scott's Strand Hotel, which stood on the corner of Clarke and Kyle streets. The two-storey building to the right of the hotel was Johnston Brothers' General Store.

School Days

Port Moody's first school opened on May 1, 1884, with an enrolment of 30 children. The community's first accredited teacher was Miss A.S. Howay, sister of one of B.C.'s best-known judges, F.W. Howay. Miss Howay was paid $50 per month.

Between 1908 and 1910, the four-room Port Moody Central School, pictured in Timms' photograph, was built on the corner of St. Johns and Moody streets. For some years after the school was built, students who wanted to go on to high school had to go to New Westminster.

The HOMES CROWD OUT THE STUMPS PORT MOODY, B.C. TIMMS

Home is Where the Heart Is

Even though prospects looked bleak, many people stayed on in Port Moody after it was known that the CPR's terminus was going to be Vancouver, not their community, which was born of both hope and avarice. As the 20th century opened, lumbering had come into its own, and a decade later the oil-refining industry proved itself there to stay. Both offered jobs for those who chose to remain in Port Moody. The cottages pictured were home to the children standing in the road. Judging by the landscape, one thing is certain—no one had to build adventure playgrounds for the kids!

"Downtown"

In 1910 most of Port Moody's shops and businesses were located on Clarke Street. In the foreground on the corner of Clarke and Queen stood the 1907 Tourist Hotel. While the *B.C. Directory* for 1910 lists only one man—John Jones—as a Port Moody bartender, it would not be unreasonable to suspect that a number of those listed as "hotel keepers" and "hotel proprietors" doubled in the less prestigious role of bartender in the town's hotels. After all, it was their drinking guests who paid the bills!

16. A Railway Crossing.   Port Moody, B. C.

From Another Angle

Front and centre is the Queen Street railway crossing. Talk about a view! Practically everyone living in Port Moody 100 years ago could see the passing trains. By 1908 train watchers were kept busy with two transcontinental trains a day, one to St. Paul (Soo Line), one to Seattle (via Mission and Huntington/Sumas, where it met up with the Union Pacific), one Agassiz local, and five to Mission. In addition to all those passenger trains—double their number because they travelled both to and from Vancouver—add 30 or more freight trains that passed through Port Moody every day (or night) for a very full train-watching program. Note the Tourist Hotel just across the street.

PART OF THE
OIL WORKS
PORT MOODY B C
Timms

Oil Refineries

The eastern end of Burrard Inlet is still the site of a number of sizable oil refineries. The first to be built was that of the British Columbia Oil Refining Company Limited, incorporated on September 9, 1908. It stood just to the west of Port Moody on the site occupied by the original CPR station. In fact, the original old station became the refinery's waterfront office, while a powerhouse, refinery and storage tanks were built on the hillside above the CPR's tracks. When the plant opened it had a staff of 25.

By 1912 a cargo of 25,000 barrels of oil was arriving each month from California for refining. The plant produced high-grade lubricating oils and other petroleum products.

RECOLLECTIONS OF PORT MOODY B. C.

Lumber Saved the Day

It is no exaggeration to say that Port Moody owes its continuing existence to lumber and shingle mills. While the first mill was that of John Tiffin's Pioneer Lumber Company, which was incorporated in 1880 and remained in operation until 1891, the largest was that of the Canadian Pacific Lumber Company, which became an incorporated company on February 2, 1900.

Canadian Pacific Lumber—no relation to the railway on which the town had pinned all its hopes—initially employed 125 men. They were of many nationalities: 80 Chinese, 34 Europeans from many countries, 6 East Indians and 5 Japanese. Rates of pay reflected race, with Whites receiving $2.25, Japanese and East Indians $1.95, and Chinese $1.85 per day. The men worked 10-hour shifts, 6 days a week. The Canadian Pacific Lumber Company's buildings were destroyed by fire in 1904, and immediately replaced by new ones that housed much more up-to-date machinery. As pictured, the mill was quite impressive.

A Friendly Monster

A large donkey engine sits on a float made of logs opposite Port Moody. It may have been used to break up log booms, moving the logs to where they could be fed into the mill, or it may have been waiting to be moved upcoast to a floating logging camp, where it would have been used to bring logs out of the woods down to the saltchuck.

SAFETY FIRST

Knowing they were protected by a police force that upheld the law without fear or favour and by a fire department that was one of the world's finest, Vancouver's early citizens generally felt safe on the streets and in their homes.

Burrard Inlet's first government agent and constable was Tomkins Brew. Soon after he was appointed, his job suddenly became more demanding, when "Gassy Jack" Deighton opened his Globe Saloon just west of Hastings Mill in 1867. Deighton's watering hole was a great success, and soon the community known as Gastown grew up around the pub.

In May 1869 Brew wrote to the Colonial Secretary in London outlining his problems and asking that a police station, jail and a residence for the local constable be built in Gastown. Brew's request was granted: a cottage close to Gassy Jack's saloon was built for him, and a two-cell log lock-up was erected in the constable's back garden.

By 1871 Brew no longer felt able to cope with his many responsibilities, and was replaced by the 38-year old Jonathan Miller. The new man served efficiently as the community's only policeman for the next 15 years. When Vancouver was granted city status in 1886, the first elected council offered to make him chief of police. He declined the invitation and became, instead, Vancouver's postmaster. The police job was then offered to John Stewart, who accepted the position. Since 1883 Stewart had been the local merchants' hired night watchman who, among other tasks, turned off the gas lamps illuminating their window displays.

On May 28, 1886, Vancouver's Volunteer Hose Company No. 1 was formed. By June 2 that year a hook-and-ladder company had also been formed. The question of buying a fire engine of some sort was still being discussed when the whole city burned to the ground on Sunday, June 13. Not surprisingly, once the town had gone up in flames, little time was given to further discussion and a steam pumper costing $3,600 was bought from the John D. Ronald Company of Brussels, Ontario. (The city's first motorized vehicle—a Seagrave hose wagon—was purchased in 1907.)

Rebuilding took place quickly after the fire, and a two-storey wooden building that served as city hall, police station, jail and meeting hall was put up on Powell Street. In 1903 an attractive purpose-built police court and jail was erected on Cordova Street.

Philip Timms photographed not only the police and their station house, but also the city's firemen, their fire engines and halls, and some of the fires they fought as well.

By 1912 Vancouver's fire department had 157 men working out of 11 fire halls. In that same year it was ranked with London and Leipzig as "the world's best in efficiency and equipment." Much of the credit for the fire department's world-class status goes to the man who was its chief from 1886 until 1928, John H. Carlisle.

The City's Second Police Station

In 1903 a new building was designed for the police department by Dalton & Eveleigh, a leading Vancouver architectural firm at the time. It was located on East Cordova between Westminster Avenue (now Main Street) and Gore Avenue. As were so many Edwardian buildings, it was a hodge-podge of earlier architectural styles. Regardless, it was an attractive building with a certain "presence."

The police moved into their new building in 1904. It had three storeys, and in addition to providing space for the police courts, could accommodate "guests" in 40 steel cells: 27 for those charged as criminals, 12 for drunks and 1 for the mentally disturbed—the proverbial padded cell, one assumes. There was separate accommodation for women prisoners.

The building was torn down and a much bigger (and less attractive) police station was built on the same site and opened in 1913. The 1903 station pictured here had a much less intimidating look than the fortress-like structure that replaced it. Someone seeing it for the first time might have mistaken it for a small, rather attractive public school.

Duty Calls

Constable Keeler Fulton is on duty in front of English Bay's bathhouse on a fine summer's day in either 1907 or 1908. The constable, warmly buttoned into his heavy serge uniform and his head well protected by his bobby's helmet, patrolled the beach, keeping an eye out for lawbreakers. Their number would have included pickpockets, those drinking from their hip flasks that shone in the midday sun, and those whose bathing costumes did not, as the law required, cover them from neck to knee. As Gilbert and Sullivan put it, "A policeman's lot was not a happy one," particularly at English Bay in the middle of summer!

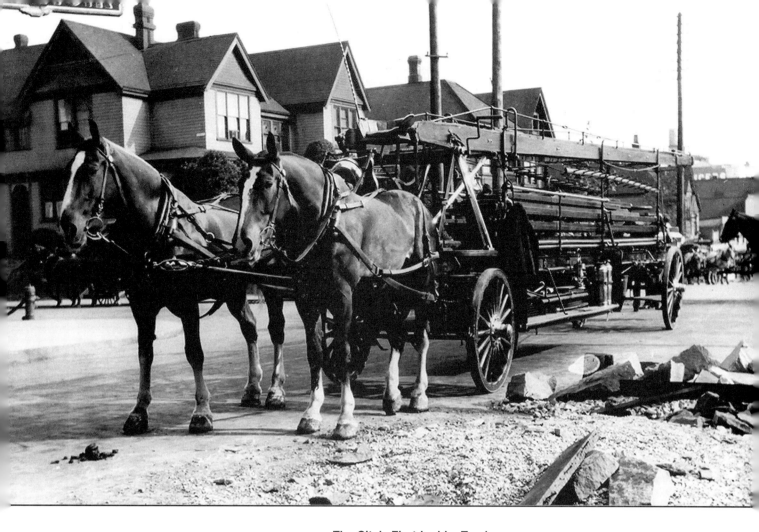

The City's First Ladder Truck

Vancouver's first horse-drawn aerial ladder truck, costing $3,400, was an 1899 Hayes, manufactured by the Waterous Engine Works Company of Brantford, Ontario. It was put into service on October 31, 1899, at Number Two Fire Hall on Seymour Street.

In July 1911 the ladders were shortened to a total length of 60 feet —perhaps because when they were fully extended, they became unstable. The ladder truck was never equipped with a hitch so that it could be towed by a motorized apparatus. It was taken out of service in 1916 and its fate after that is unknown.

The purchase of a motorized Seagrave 75-foot aerial ladder in 1909, and a motorized Webb front-wheel drive, 85-foot aerial ladder in 1912, marked the end of the era of the horse-drawn ladder truck like the 1899 Hayes pictured here.

Steam Pumpers

Before the days of the motorized fire truck, most of Vancouver's fire engines were produced by two Ontario firms, the John D. Ronald Company of Brussels and the Waterous Engine Works of Brantford.

In the late 19th and early 20th centuries the steam pumper was an essential piece of firefighting equipment. If a fire hydrant was near the site of a fire, the pumper's 2½-inch-diameter hose would be attached to it. The flow of water was drawn into the steam pump by reciprocating pistons and the water was discharged through the hose at 50 to 100 pounds of pressure per square inch. The desired pressure was determined by the size and type of hose and nozzle being used to fight a particular fire. As can be seen in Timms' postcard, the pumper carried a rigid, four-to-six-inch "hard suction" hose that could be used when no hydrant was close by and water had to be taken from a cistern, well or stream.

Each steam pumper had an engineer whose job it was to get up steam in a hurry. There was always warmed water in the boiler, so that when an alarm came in to the fire hall, all the engineer had to do was light the kindling in the pumper's firebox and get the wood or coal fire going. Ideally, by the time the steamer got to the scene of the fire, it would be producing sufficient steam to power the pistons that pumped the water needed to put out the fire.

Between 1886 and 1908 Vancouver's fire department had put seven horse-drawn steam pumpers into service. While the city's first two steam pumps were originally pulled along by manpower, all the later, larger and much heavier pumpers were drawn by horses, harnessed either as two- or three-horse teams, depending on the weight of the wagon being drawn.

When the fire department became fully motorized in 1917—the first to do so in North America—the newer steam pumps were equipped with hitches, so that when it became necessary to use them, they could be pulled along by motorized vehicles. In 1914 a motorized fire engine built by American LaFrance was put into service. Its pump was a Type 15, powered by a gasoline engine that could pump 1,250 gallons per minute. Such motorized fire engines meant that steam pumpers would soon become history. The last steam pumper on the city's roster of fire-fighting equipment was kept in storage behind Fire Hall No.13, at 24th Avenue and Prince Albert, until the early 1940s.

An Ever-Present Danger

In the years before the Second World War, Vancouver was a fire waiting to happen. False Creek was ringed by sawmills, sash and door factories, shingle mills and any number of businesses that produced wood products—things like packing cases and barrels, for example. As well, hundreds of thousands of board feet of dressed lumber were exported annually by ship or rail. Lumber kilns, beehive burners and careless smokers meant that the risk of a major fire breaking out in Vancouver was always a distinct possibility. Thanks to the Vancouver fire department's skill and experience, however, the city never had to face a second "Great Fire."

By 1912 Chief J.H. Carlisle had a fire department of 157 officers and men, and he was continually upgrading equipment. Doubtless a few eyebrows were raised when, in the same year, both the chief and the sub-chief were supplied with "motors." In 1912 the fire brigade had 8 miles of 2½-inch-diameter hose, over 1,100 fire hydrants ready for use and 216 Gamewell fire-alarm boxes on the city streets. Vancouver was one of the first cities in North America to have installed these automatic call boxes. By 1912 over $1 million had been invested in firefighting equipment, and over $200,000 was being spent annually on the department.

Even though Vancouver only extended southward as far as 16th Avenue in 1913, it already had 14 fire halls. The city also had two full-time fire wardens equipped with motorcycles whose job it was to continually patrol the city's business and factory districts.

Fire on Seymour Street

Philip Timms took pictures of a number of serious fires in the years before the Great War of 1914–1918. While he rarely recorded the dates or mentioned the locations of the conflagrations he photographed, this postcard view is dated 1906 and the fire is identified as being in the 600-block Seymour Street. He took this particular shot from a Granville Street rooftop, looking toward Seymour Street with its mix of substantial, late-Victorian homes and newer commercial properties.

Long since demolished, one of the principal landmarks visible on the right in the postcard is St. Andrew's Presbyterian Church. First opened on May 25, 1890, it stood on the northeast corner of Georgia and Richards. The huge Carpenter Gothic church was designed by William Blackmore, the architect who in 1888 had prepared the plans for the congregation's first and much more modest church on Melville Street. The building became redundant when the new St. Andrew's Wesley United Church on Burrard Street brought the congregations of St. Andrew's Presbyterian and Wesley Methodist together under one roof.

On the left, at the north end of the 600-block Richards Street, another landmark, Holy Rosary Roman Catholic Cathedral, towers over its neighbours. Designed by Thomas E. Julian, the church was built in 1899–1900 in the Gothic Revival style. It replaced a much smaller 1889 building, the square tower of which can be seen to the right of the present-day cathedral.

ENGLISH BAY

E nglish Bay was named by Captain George Vancouver in June 1792. Perhaps he chose the name to underscore the British presence in the area and, as it were, to put the Spaniards in their place. Fast-forwarding 100 years, Vancouver's name for the bay seemed most appropriate. English Bay was just that—an English seaside resort in Canada's far west.

English Bay was no Blackpool, but it did have its attractions. Prior to 1905, when the beach came under the Parks Board's control and regulations, there had been much haphazard, unattractive and undesirable development on the beach. Not only were there ramshackle, privately owned bathing pavilions providing changing rooms on their ground floors and refreshment parlours on their upper floors, there was the English Bay Club—a men-only social club. There were boat rentals, a giant waterslide and refreshment stands. To the east were a number of camps, that is, tent colonies set up by local families for the summer months. A family camp could consist of tents for sleeping, a tent that could serve as a parlour/dining room and a tent that could be used as a kitchen. While sanitation was questionable and water safety less than ideal, camping in those days didn't necessarily mean roughing it.

As soon as English Bay came under the control of the Parks Board, improvements were instituted. In its natural state the beach was covered in rocks, seaweed and barnacles. In the first year that English Bay was the Parks Board's responsibility, the narrow beach, which had been cleared of rocks, was considerably expanded. The first publicly owned bathhouse was built in 1907. It was in the usual style of the day, with changing rooms on the lower floor, and space on the upper floor for a band and spectators. Also completed in 1907 was the pier at the west end of the beach, built at a cost of $21,000. J.E. Parr and T.A. Fee were its architects.

English Bay was very popular and accessible to everyone; those who lived in the West End and what is now the downtown area could easily walk to the beach, while those who lived farther away could get there by streetcar. Tenting on the public beach was no longer allowed, and in 1911 the Parks Board set out to buy up all the waterfront properties along Beach Avenue. The final parcels of land were not acquired until the 1980s. Today, thanks to the farsightedness of the Parks Board nearly a century ago, all who walk or drive along Beach Avenue have an unobstructed view of English Bay and beyond.

Joe Fortes

Joe Fortes is pictured here diving at English Bay. After he surfaced he probably encouraged the three boys, who look less than enthusiastic, to have a go at it, too. Born in the West Indies, Fortes went to sea in his youth and arrived in Vancouver aboard the *Robert Kerr* in 1885. The ship was deemed no longer seaworthy, so Fortes settled in Vancouver, where he built a small cottage down at English Bay.

By 1890 he had begun teaching the youngsters at the beach how to swim, and at the same time looked out for their safety. In 1900 Joe Fortes became Vancouver's first paid lifeguard and swimming instructor. He was also the English Bay constable. By the time he died on February 4, 1922, he was known by virtually everyone in town. His funeral was paid for by the city in appreciation of his life of service to Vancouver and its children. A memorial drinking fountain designed by Charles Marega stands across from English Bay beach in Alexandra Park. The apt inscription reads "Little Children Loved Him."

339. *Among the Canoists, English Bay. Vancouver, B. C.*

Fools March In …

English Bay always drew huge crowds in the summer, with boating being a particularly popular attraction. Of the 20 or so boaters pictured—all in their finest "summer casual" dress—not one had a life jacket. And it would be safe to bet that at least a third of their number couldn't swim a stroke.

Boating at English Bay

Boating was immensely popular with both the Victorians and the Edwardians. And didn't they dress for the sport! In this Timms photograph we see the women in their uniforms—white lawn blouses with leg-of-mutton sleeves, straw hats and full, dark skirts—and the men in their prescribed costumes—suits, ties and either a bowler or a boater on their heads. Doubtless many a summer romance blossomed on the waters of English Bay.

"Our Bathing Beach"

Timms' postcard, dating from 1907, certainly doesn't suggest that English Bay was one of the city's beauty spots. An assortment of buildings lined the narrow length of beach, from which stones and boulders had been cleared. On the left of the photo are two privately owned bathhouses, the Pavilion and the Crescent. Behind them stood the men-only English Bay Club. Just to the right of the private facilities in the centre of the photo were the bathhouse and pavilion that the city built in 1907. Farther east, private homes lined the waterfront along Beach Avenue.

A Great Photo

Philip Timms had an eye for the evocative as he photographed Vancouver in the years before the Great War. By 1911 nearly 74 percent of Vancouver's residents were of British origin. While it may not have been Henley or even the Thames, the English fondness for boating is well reflected in this scene at English Bay.

VICTORIOUS VISITORS

On February 8, 1904, Japan launched a surprise torpedo attack on Russia's Pacific Squadron stationed at Port Arthur, or Lüshun, as the harbour was called by the Chinese. The Japanese action was the opening salvo in what came to be known as the Russo-Japanese War. The war grew out of the rivalry between Russia and Japan for control of Korea and Manchuria. Japan needed easy access to China with its vast reserves of iron and coal, while Russia felt it had to secure a southern branch line across Manchuria from Ulan Ude in Siberia to the deep ice-free harbour at Port Arthur for its Trans-Siberian railway. Port Arthur, named by the British Navy in 1860 after one of its captains, William Arthur, is strategically located at the southern tip of Manchuria's Liaotung Peninsula. To the east, across the Yellow Sea, the peninsula separates China from Korea. Port Arthur is located at the narrow entrance to the Gulf of Bohai to the west, making it the ocean gateway to Beijing, which lies along the western shore of the gulf.

Although Russia had agreed in 1903 to withdraw its troops from Manchuria, it had not done so. Because the Russians would not honour their commitment, the Japanese launched their naval attack on Port Arthur. At the same time they landed an army in Korea and occupied China's Liaotung Peninsula, effectively cutting off the Russians' land route to Port Arthur. Each side's losses were heavy: during the battle of March 1905 at Mukden—the last engagement on land—Russian casualties numbered 89,000 and Japanese losses were 71,000.

Significant though the land battles were, the war's deciding battle was fought at sea. On October 15, 1904, Russia's Baltic Fleet set sail for the Far East to relieve Port Arthur. While Admiral Zinovy Petrovich Rozhestvensky's fleet was formidable, many of his ships were old and their crews not well trained. Reaching the China Sea in early May 1905, Rozhestvensky made for Vladivostok by way of the Tsushima Strait. Laying in wait off the Korean coast near Puson was the Japanese fleet commanded by Admiral Togo Heihachiro. On May 27, as the Russian fleet came into sight, he attacked.

The Japanese ships were superior in every way, and within 48 hours, two-thirds of the Russian warships were sunk and six more were captured. Only four Russian ships reached Vladivostok, while six others took refuge in neutral ports. On September 5, 1905, thanks to the good offices of American president Theodore Roosevelt, a peace settlement was signed. In the Treaty of Portsmouth, Russia recognized Japan as the dominant power in Korea, and turned its leases to Port Arthur and the Liaotung Peninsula over to the Japanese. Japan also acquired control of the southern half of Sakhalin Island. Both powers agreed to recognize China's sovereignty in Manchuria.

The Russo-Japanese War left Imperial Russia humiliated and ripe for the October Revolution that led to the granting by Nicolas II of a constitution of sorts. Japan emerged from the war as a world power and Britain's principal Asian ally. On their way to the June 1, 1909, opening of Seattle's Alaska–Yukon Pacific Exhibition, two Japanese cruisers that had formerly been ships of the Imperial Russian Navy visited Vancouver from May 17 until May 21. The vessels not only said much about the new Japan to Vancouver's White population, but enhanced the stature of the province's Japanese in the eyes of their neighbours.

"Britains' Ally" entering Western Gate.   Vancouver, B. C.

A Ship of the Line

On the morning of May 17, 1909, the *Aso* and the *Soya*, two cruisers that belonged to His Imperial Japanese Majesty's navy arrived in Vancouver for a five-day visit. They were being used as cadet training ships and had come up the coast from San Francisco, stopping at other ports, including Esquimalt, en route to their most northerly port of call. Both had been Russian naval vessels stationed at Port Arthur with the First Pacific Squadron when the Russo-Japanese War broke out in early 1904. The *Aso* is pictured passing through the First Narrows. The *Soya* entered the harbour a little later in the day.

The *Aso* was formerly the Russian navy's armed cruiser *Bayan*. Because all the Russian yards were already working at full capacity in 1902–03, the ship was built in a French shipyard at La Seyne. Of a new design, with a maximum speed of 21 knots and a range of 7,000 nautical miles at 10 knots, the *Aso* was well suited to fulfill its primary purpose, which was to seek out and destroy enemy merchant ships.

On July 27, 1904, the *Bayan* struck a Japanese mine but made it back to Port Arthur, where it was scuttled to avoid capture. After the war it was raised, refitted and renamed *Aso* by the Japanese. The cruiser served as a ship of the line until 1932, when it was used as a target in a training exercise and sunk.

"Banzai." "Banzai." "Banzai." The Admiral and his Retinue.
Vancouver, B. C.

Patriotic Pride

The two Japanese cruisers arrived in Vancouver on Monday, May 17, to a tumultuous welcome from the Lower Mainland's Japanese population. Their 1909 visit to several North and South American west-coast ports underscored Japan's new-found place in the sun. While their principal port of call was to be Seattle, where they were to be present at the official opening of the Alaska–Yukon–Pacific Exhibition, nowhere did they receive a warmer welcome than in Vancouver.

Philip Timms' postcard, rather patronizingly entitled "The Admiral and his Retinue," pictures a group of Japanese children dressed in their finest. In all probability they and their teachers were waiting to be ferried out to the warships anchored in Burrard Inlet. On the Tuesday and Wednesday of their visit, the ships were open to the public. From 10 o'clock in the morning, overloaded launches sailed between shore and the cruisers until late in the afternoon.

The North Vancouver Ferry Commission allowed vessels carrying passengers to and from the visiting ships to use its ferry slip, provided 5¢ was paid to the commission for every passenger embarking from the ferry slip. As the *Daily Province* suggested, every Japanese person who could possibly manage it "deemed it his sacred duty to visit the cruisers." The local Japanese community was hospitality itself, holding a reception for officers and crew from one until five on the afternoons of May 18 and 19.

A Checkered History

Timms pictures the *Aso* and the *Soya* riding at anchor in Burrard Inlet. By the time the ships had reached their destination they were surrounded by over 100 Japanese fishing boats from both Vancouver and Steveston. The *Soya,* seen in the foreground with its flag fluttering, was built for the Russians in Philadelphia, and launched in 1901 as the *Varyag*. Like the *Aso,* it was coal-burning, and though slightly smaller, had a top speed of 23 knots. Severely damaged in battle in February 1904, the ship managed to make it back to Port Arthur, where it was scuttled at its moorings. Japan's Admiral Arai had the vessel raised and repaired. While the rehabilitation of the vessel cost more than the price of a new cruiser, in the eyes of the Japanese the potential propaganda value of the captured and refitted *Varyag* cum *Soya,* made the exercise fully worthwhile.

One of history's little ironies is that in April 1916 the cruiser was sold back to the Russian government and again became the *Varyag*. Urgently requiring repairs, the vessel arrived in Liverpool in February 1917. It was still in Britain when the 1917 revolution broke out in Russia, and was, therefore, seized by the Royal Navy. Stationed off Liverpool as a hulk in 1923, the former cruiser broke loose from its moorings, ran aground and was stranded. No longer of any real use, the vessel was sold to a German firm for scrap.

SCHOOLS AND MORE SCHOOLS

Vancouver began as a settlement that grew up around Hastings Mill, which came into operation in 1865. By 1872 the settlement included 15 to 20 schoolaged children; the time had come to elect a board of school trustees. Its first matter of business was to build a school. Lumber was donated by the mill, and an 18-by-44-foot schoolhouse was soon erected. The school, along with nearly every other building in the newly incorporated City of Vancouver, was destroyed in the Great Fire of June 13, 1886.

A new, two-storey frame schoolhouse was built on Cordova Street, just east of Jackson Avenue. It had four classrooms and cost $3,000 to build. In 1887 a second four-room school was built on the corner of Burrard and Barclay in what was known as the West End, and a two-room school was built on the south side of False Creek in what would become Mount Pleasant. The growing need for classrooms did not abate, and so in 1888 the city's first eight-room school—Central School—was built on Pender Street between Cambie and Hamilton. The building was the city's first "permanent" school, meaning it was built of brick.

In the years immediately before the Great War, Vancouver grew by leaps and bounds, and the expanding population called for more schools to be built. Between 1889 and 1913 a further 29 new schools were erected, 18 of them between 1909 and 1913. All of these newer schools had no fewer than eight classrooms. In 1910 the first schools built of concrete—Nelson, Cecil Rhodes and Tennyson—were put up. As was the style at the time, they were clad in brick veneer.

A School of Many Names (top right)

Designed by Dalton and Eveleigh, one of Vancouver's most attractive schools stood between Yew and Vine streets on West 4th Avenue. Built in 1904, the eight-room school reflected the dictates of the English Arts and Craft Movement, which was very popular at the time. It opened on January 5, 1905, as Fairview West. From 1906 until 1932 it was known as Kitsilano Public School, and from 1932 until 1935 it was called Seaview School. In 1935 the building became the Fairview High School of Commerce Annex. It continued as such until 1943, when it was no long needed as an overflow facility by the Fairview High School of Commerce.

The building was taken over in 1943 by the Royal Canadian Air Force, which used it as a training centre. When the war ended, the building, once again called Seaview School, was being used by the federal Canadian Vocational Training program. Some 450 Second World War veterans completed their junior matriculation at Seaview and consequently became eligible for admission to the University of British Columbia.

Unfortunately, arson ended the program at Seaview. At 6.24 a.m. on January 1, 1947, a fire alarm was sent in from a street fire-alarm call box. By 8:00 a.m. the frame building was a total loss. After the fire, the classes for ex-servicemen and women were relocated to empty army huts at Little Mountain Camp.

Grandview High School of Commerce

Just as the Fairview High School of Commerce evolved out of the commercial program offered at King Edward High School, so the Grandview High School of Commerce started life in 1913 as Britannia High School's department of commerce. In 1926 its five classes were moved from Britannia to Charles Dickens School (18th Avenue and Glen Drive). From there, it moved in the spring of 1927 to the Grand View (*sic*) Elementary School's old building at First and Commercial. In 1932 Britannia's commercial department became the Grandview High School of Commerce, and in 1950 the commercial school was consolidated with Vancouver Technical School, and the school at First and Commercial closed. The building was demolished in 1954. Timms' picture of the school (right) was taken not long after it was built in 1905.

The Model School

Designed by E.E. "Ted" Blackmore, the Model School on 12th Avenue off Cambie was built in 1905. Blackmore was a clever architect with wide talents who designed everything from Chinese laundries to the bandstand in Stanley Park. The Model School was built of stone and brick and had 10 classrooms. Its style was described as "Late Victorian Eclectic."

For three years, the Model School accommodated the Provincial Normal School, which had opened in 1901 in temporary quarters in the city's high school. It had 42 students. A lack of space in the schools of the day forced the Normal School to move a number of times before it got its own building. In 1902 it was at Lord Roberts in the West End, in 1905 it returned to the high school, and in 1906 it was accommodated in the brand-new Model School. In 1909 it moved into its own building next door to the Model School. At the time it had a staff of six: a principal, two assistant masters, an art master, an instructor in nature study and a drill instructor.

In 1911 A.M. Ross wrote that "the Model School was a large public school where specially selected teachers are in charge … and where the Normal students are permitted to observe and to teach under the direction of the regular Model teachers, and the members of the Normal [School] staff."

The Normal School closed in 1956, when all would-be teachers in British Columbia took their training at the University of British Columbia. It was not that many years before changing demographics brought about the closure of the Model School. Fortunately, both buildings have been preserved and function as integral parts of an attractive and imaginatively designed shopping mall.

Vancouver High School

It was not until January 1890 that Vancouver had enough students of high-school age to consider offering a secondary school program. At that time a room was provided for future high-school students in Central School. By 1893 there were enough elementary students who were ready to attend high school to make the construction of an eight-room high school worthwhile—so worthwhile that 10 years later it could not accommodate any more students.

In 1907 the school board bought seven acres in Fairview for $6,500 as a site for a new high school. The acreage was bounded by Oak and Laurel between 10th and 12th avenues. The new Vancouver High School's architect was William T. Whiteway, a Newfoundlander who had established himself as a popular Vancouver designer. While he specialized in designs for schools—he had produced the plans for at least six for the city—he had other claims to fame. Whiteway was the architect for Woodward's first Hastings Street store, the Kelly, Douglas building, and his crowning glory, the World (Sun) Tower. The school opened on January 5, 1905. Even though it had 20 classrooms, it wasn't long before it had to be enlarged, and a 10-room addition was built in 1912 along its 12th Avenue side.

The school became King Edward High School on May 24, 1910. Since the city had built a second high school in 1909—Britannia—the original school could no longer simply be called "Vancouver High School." Sadly, King Edward High School was destroyed by fire on June 19, 1973. Fortunately, the building was no longer being used as a high school: in 1962 it had been replaced by Eric Hamber Secondary School at West 33rd and Oak. When it burned, the building was being used as a somewhat makeshift adult-education centre. That centre evolved into Vancouver City College (now at Langara campus) and the old school's property provided a much-needed site for the expansion of the Vancouver General Hospital.

Burrard Inlet

THE NORTH SHORE

Moodyville was the first non-Aboriginal settlement on the North Shore of Burrard Inlet. It had come into being in the early 1860s when its waterfront site—now occupied by the Saskatchewan Wheat Pool's grain elevator—was pre-empted for a sawmill. The mill, built by J.W. Graham and George Scrimgeour, did not become a success until 1865, when it passed into the hands of Sewell "Sue" Prescott Moody, an American from Maine. The mill flourished until the end of the 19th century, when a changing economic climate and stiff competition from mills in False Creek and along the Fraser River, and from Hastings Mill across the Inlet, forced the Moodyville mill to close in 1901.

As Moodyville's fortunes were fading, a community was developing on both sides of what later became lower Lonsdale Avenue. By 1900 the settlement had a population of more than 100 White residents, who petitioned the lieutenant-governor for incorporation as a district municipality. The new municipality—North Vancouver —covered over 100 square miles of land running from the waterfront to the mountains between Horseshoe Bay and Deep Cove.

While there were pockets of settlement throughout the municipality in places like Lynn Valley and Capilano, it wasn't long before the principal centre of North Vancouver was Lonsdale Avenue. In 1900 a reliable, scheduled ferry service between downtown Vancouver and the foot of Lonsdale was inaugurated by the *Norvan*. Increasingly, North Vancouver was showing potential as a residential community. By 1909 there were already 23 local real estate companies recruiting potential residents. The gem at the centre of the realtors' diadem was the 12-block-long, 346-foot-wide Grand Boulevard. Locals proudly proclaimed it the longest and widest boulevard in the world.

The 1900s were salad days for North Vancouver. By 1911 there were at least 11 lumber and shingle mills operating in the city and district. A streetcar service was introduced in 1906 by B.C. Electric. Its lines ran from the ferry slip to both Lynn Valley and Capilano. The community was growing quickly—by 1905 there were already over 2,500 people living in the Lonsdale area—and it felt a need to incorporate as a city, leaving its country cousins to fend for themselves. The City of North Vancouver was incorporated on May 13, 1907, and prospered until 1913, when a worldwide depression grounded many an enterprise and ended the local real estate boom.

Twenty years later, the Great Depression hit North Vancouver with a vengeance, forcing the city into receivership in 1933. It was not until 1944 that it was once again solvent and able to manage its own affairs. Following the Second World War, both the city of North Vancouver and the district municipality of North Vancouver came into their own, at last fulfilling the dreams of those who, half a century earlier, had promised a bright, secure future for those who lived and worked on the North Shore.

The Mission

The first people to live along the North Shore of Burrard Inlet were of the Coast Salish Nation. While no one knows just how long the Salish have lived in the area, they were certainly there in the 18th century to greet both the Spaniards and the British, who were busily exploring and charting the coast of today's British Columbia.

Indian Reserve Number 1, usually called "the Mission" by non-Natives and *Ustlawn* by the indigenous people, is a few blocks west of Lonsdale along the shores and estuary of Mosquito Creek.

The missionaries who first brought the Gospel to the community were the Oblates of Mary Immaculate, who built a temporary chapel on the site in 1866. It was the first Roman Catholic place of worship built in what is now Greater Vancouver. The chapel was replaced by a church with a single spire, *l'Eglise de Notre-Dame des Sept Douleurs,* in 1884. It can be seen on the right in Timms' photograph of the reserve that dates from 1905 or 1906.

In 1909 the building was extensively remodelled, gaining twin spires in place of the single tower. As well, transepts were added to the nave. The renovated church gained a credible neo-Gothic look and is an important heritage landmark today. At the time of its renovation it was renamed "St. Paul's" in honour of the diocesan bishop Paul Durieu, the driving force behind the Roman Catholic church's 19th-century mission to the local First Nations people.

The North Vancouver Ferry Service

Until the Second Narrows Bridge opened in 1925, the only way to get to the North Shore was to sail or swim. Most people unquestionably preferred to sail the two and a half miles from the foot of Vancouver's Columbia Street to the foot of Lonsdale Avenue in North Vancouver.

While a reliable and scheduled ferry service had been introduced in 1899–1900 by the district municipality, it had limitations. The vessel designed and built for the job—the *Norvan*—loaded from the side. This meant that when the horse-drawn wagons of the day were loaded on board, considerable time-consuming manoeuvring was necessary. To complicate matters more, the little ferry could only accommodate smaller wagons.

In 1903 along came Lieutenant Colonel Alfred St. George Hamersley, K.C., who was a lawyer and something of an adventurer. Among other roles, he acted as Vancouver's city solicitor beginning in 1888. Detractors observed that beneath the high-sounding name and impeccable British credentials was just another land speculator and stock promoter. Regardless, in 1903 Hamersley incorporated (in Ontario) the North Vancouver Ferry and Power Company, and then approached North Vancouver's council, offering to take over the municipality's money-losing ferry service. Needless to say, the ratepayers happily turned the ferry service over to Hamersley.

Hamersley's design for his first and, as it turned out, only ferry was presented to council and approved on November 16, 1903. The *St. George* was well-designed for its job. It was a 131-foot-long, double-ended ship that could cross Burrard Inlet in less than 20 minutes. Prefabricated in Collingwood, Ontario, it was shipped to Wallace Shipyard on False Creek for assembly. It was an elegant vessel providing every comfort, including separate restrooms for ladies and gentlemen.

Perhaps not unexpectedly, in 1907 Hamersley announced that he was discontinuing what had again proven to be a money-losing ferry service. The municipality had no choice but to buy the *St. George* and run the service itself. The North Van ferries operated as a public utility until the last vessel completed its final trip on August 30, 1958. Hamersley returned to England, where he became a Conservative Member of Parliament.

On the Waterfront

Philip Timms took this picture of North Vancouver's waterfront from the deck of one of the city's ferries. By 1912—the presumed date of this photograph—three ferries were in service: the original *Norvan*, which can be seen docked to the left of the ferry slip at the foot of Lonsdale, the *St. George*, renamed *North Vancouver Ferry No. 2*, and *North Vancouver Ferry No. 3*, launched in 1911.

Timms' photo shows the community as it began to take on the look of a city: stone and brick business blocks and hotels are replacing the village's original shingle and clapboard structures. By 1912 North Vancouver had two sizable hotels; one was the red-brick Palace Hotel. Built in 1906 on East 2nd Street, half a block east of Lonsdale, it advertised that it not only had over 100 rooms renting at $2 a day, but was also the only hotel in British Columbia to have a roof garden. It later became the Olympic, "the Big O," with a beer parlour well known to many making their way home after a day's work in the shipyard or mills. The other "name" hotel in North Vancouver was the St. Alice. It opened in 1912 on West 2nd, just off Lonsdale, and had been named by its owner, Antonio Gallia, after his wife. In its later years the St. Alice Hotel, which had a number of self-contained suites, became a residential hotel providing a home to single working men. Both hotels can be seen in Tiimms' postcard view, and, as it happened, both were demolished in 1989 to make room for high-rise condominiums.

To the right of the ferry slip, Wallace Shipyard can be seen. The firm was first established in False Creek in 1892 and did not relocate to North Vancouver until 1903. Andrew Wallace originally purchased land in North Vancouver with 350 feet of waterfront. He also had a Crown grant extending his water lot 600 feet beyond the high-water mark out into the harbour. In 1912 his shipyard employed 250 men and its payroll was close to $12,000 per month—big wages in those days. The ship in dry dock was probably a CPR costal steamer. At the time Wallace had the contract to convert four of the company's vessels from coal-burning to oil-fired ships.

In 1921 the firm was renamed Burrard Drydock, and in 1971 the Wallace family sold out to what would in 1978 become Versatile Pacific Shipyards. Time proved the firm to be somewhat less versatile than its name suggested, and in 1992 the business closed, laying off its last employees. As the 21st century begins, the shipyard's site is being redeveloped as a waterfront residential complex that will include a number of high-rise (and high-cost) condos. Such is progress.

Central School

Built in 1902, this very attractive school was originally known as North Vancouver School. While it is now all but unrecognizable, the building still stands on the west side of Chesterfield Avenue between 3rd and 4th streets. Timms' 1907 picture shows the building being enlarged through the addition of two new classrooms. The larger schoolhouse had a pair of cupolas (possibly made of copper) that added visual importance to the addition. They appear to have been designed to match the earlier belfry that is peeking over the rooftop in Timms' photo.

With the opening of Queen Mary School in 1915, the old school—further remodelled and enlarged without any artistic or architectural sensitivity—became North Vancouver's city hall. It continued to serve as such until 1975, when it became the home of the North Vancouver Archives and Museum, and the venue for serveral community-based cultural and artistic programs.

This photo, with the horse-drawn wagon laboriously making its way up Chesterfield, is a Timms classic.

The Municipal Hall

Although North Vancouver was incorporated as a district municipality in 1891, it did not acquire a purpose-built municipal hall until 1903. The new hall, on the northwest corner of Lonsdale Avenue and 1st Street, was designed without charge by C.O. Wickenden, reeve of North Vancouver municipality from 1901 to 1903. He is remembered as one of Vancouver's most sought-after late-19th century architects. If not his best work, certainly his most lasting one has been Vancouver's Christ Church Cathedral.

On May 13, 1907, the City of North Vancouver was incorporated. Its creation, which took a large bite out of the Municipality of North Vancouver, had been actively promoted by land developers like Edward Mahon, J.C Keith and W.J. Irwin. A new municipal hall was built in Lynn Valley, and the building at Lonsdale and 1st became the new town's city hall. The celebrations marking the creation of the City of North Vancouver were delayed until July 1, 1907. Timms' postcard shows people celebrating their community's new civic status in front of the city hall.

The Hotel North Vancouver

The Hotel North Vancouver was built west of Lonsdale on the Esplanade in 1902 for Pete Larson. At the time the Esplanade was little more than a boardwalk. Larson, who was born in Sweden, began his career as a sailor. When his job brought him to Port Moody, he saw a chance for a new and better life and jumped ship. He made his way to Vancouver, where he opened the Hotel Norden on Cordova Street.

In 1901 Larson relocated to North Vancouver and had the Hotel North Vancouver built. Almost from the day it opened it became the unofficial social centre of the community. Larson was not only an astute businessman, but something of a showman as well, and made sure there was always a reason for people to gather on the Esplanade. Among other things, he started Sunday band concerts, hosted annual picnics like Vancouver's annual Butchers' Picnic, and staged events like balloon ascents and tightrope walking.

Next door to his hotel Larson built the Pavilion. It was soon a popular site for concerts, dances and political rallies. As would be expected, his hotel bar was in and of itself a popular attraction.

The Hotel North Vancouver's rates were always competitive. In 1910 they were $2 per day or $10 per week, with "special rates for Families and Steady Boarders." How steady the boarders were may have depended on how frequently they visited Larson's popular bar. With the coming of Prohibition in 1915, Larson decided it was time to retire: running a dry, money-losing hotel just wasn't much fun. The hotel was destroyed by fire in 1929.

Timms' picture postcard dates from 1905 or 1906. All the ladies, young or old, dressed alike as they are, look like they are in uniform. The wonderful wicker stroller in the foreground would be a museum piece today.

"THE LOGGING TRAIN" WEST VANCOUVER

TIMMS PHOTO CO.

Old-Growth Timber

Logging in the Capilano Valley, that is, the hundreds of acres above what is now the site of Cleveland Dam, did not begin until the early years of the 20th century. The reason the old-growth timber was not harvested at an earlier date was because there was no practical way to move the logs down to tidewater. The deep Capilano Canyon was too narrow and twisting to be used to float the huge logs to a mill, and moving them the six miles to tidewater using teams of horses or oxen was equally impractical.

In 1906 a syndicate of Bellingham lumbermen bought 4,000 acres of timbered land above the old Vancouver Waterworks dam on the Capilano River. The purchase contained an estimated 200 million board feet of lumber. The investors attempted to negotiate a deal with B.C. Electric whereby it would extend its rail line up to the old dam on the Capilano in order to move logs down to Burrard Inlet. Nothing came of the scheme, and the forested lands were sold to another Washington group, which resold the property within a month to the A.B. Nickey family of Chicago. It was their company—the Capilano Timber Company—that was ultimately to log off much of the Capilano Valley which, incidentally, was and is a watershed that provides much of Vancouver's drinking water. Capilano Timber went on to buy the Mahon family's timber licences, gaining a further 100 million board feet of timber. A mill was built near the foot of Pemberton on a 35-acre site with 675 feet of water frontage.

In 1917–1918 the Capilano Timber Company built its own eight-mile long railway from the company's sawmill on Burrard Inlet up to its timber holdings in the

Capilano Valley (much of which is now under water, serving as a huge reservoir.) Most of the line was to the west of the Capilano River and Canyon. It was a difficult route, with one trestle having to be 90 feet high and 450 feet long. In its 16 years of operation, an additional 50 miles of track were laid throughout the Capilano Valley to provide access to the trees being felled. Over 75,000 board feet of timber were taken by rail to the booming grounds daily. Logging ended in 1933, after some 400 million board feet of quality timber had been taken out of the valley. Almost immediately the Greater Vancouver Water District got what it had wanted for years: a protected watershed on the Capilano River.

Timms' postcard probably dates from 1918, and was taken at some point along the Capilano Timber Company's line in West Vancouver. The train seems to be made up of a donkey engine and some of the company's dozen or so log carriers. Note the photographer's other camera that can be seen in the photo.

159

New Westminster

THE ROYAL CITY

The crown colony of British Columbia came into existence in 1858. In 1859 Colonel Richard C. Moody of the Royal Engineers recommended a site on the north side of the Fraser River as appropriate for the colony's capital. It would be much easier to defend than Derby (Fort Langley), should the Americans pose a problem. Governor Douglas accepted Moody's advice, and Queen Victoria was asked to name the yet-to-be-created colonial capital: she chose to call it the "City of New Westminster"; its sobriquet "The Royal City" reflects the origins of its regal designation.

In 1866 the colonies of British Columbia and Vancouver Island united as British Columbia, with New Westminster as its capital. Unfortunately for the Royal City, Vancouver Island's members of the legislature took advantage of a day when numerous members from the mainland were absent from the chamber to cast their votes making Victoria the capital of the united British Columbia.

New Westminster, which is geographically at the heart of the Greater Vancouver Regional District, is a relatively small city, having a population of 55,000 living in an area of only 7.1 square miles. In its early days, salmon canneries and sawmills were the community's principal industries. One of the defining events in the early days of the city's history was the Great Fire of September 10, 1898, which destroyed much of the city. Many homes, businesses and public buildings burned to the ground. Another defining event was the opening in 1904 of the rail and road bridge that crossed the Fraser River. While it had already been serving as the Fraser Valley's market town before the bridge was built, the new road and rail link increased the city's importance as the commercial centre for the region's agricultural community.

While New Westminster speaks proudly of its past, it has not done a very good job as far as historic preservation is concerned. Thoughtless demolition of architecturally significant buildings proceeded without hindrance almost to the beginning of the present century. Fortunately, many citizens have done a great job of preserving residential properties. New Westminster can be proud of the number of beautifully restored and preserved early homes within its city limits. Interestingly, Philip Timms, one of British Columbia's finest photographers in the Golden Age of Postcards, 1900 to 1910, appreciated the unique appeal of New Westminster, and deliberately set out to photograph much that was of special interest in the Royal City. He left a legacy of over 50 photographic postcards featuring the sites that made New Westminster such an interesting and vibrant community.

The Carnegie Free Library

Along with so many other buildings, New Westminster's public library on Columbia Street was destroyed in the Great Fire of 1898. The new library building, funded in large part by a Carnegie grant, was built on the block bounded by Agnes, Lorne, Carnarvon and McKenzie streets. The block had been occupied by the city hall before the fire.

Edwin G.W. Sait designed the new library, whose cornerstone was laid on October 1, 1902. Sait must have seen the generous sloping property as an ideal site for a building in the style of Andrea Palladio (1508–1580). Palladio, an Italian, always designed his villas with reference to their setting: if on a hillside, for example, all facades were designed to be of equal value. He also followed the principles of classical Roman architecture, which was grounded in mathematical ratios for proportion. He was not interested in the popular styles of the Renaissance, which relied on rich ornamentation for their effect. Instead of an open portico or porch, Palladio often used a loggia or recessed portico—like the one on the south side of the library—for a building's entranceway. And his villas were almost invariably square.

Looking at Timms' postcard photo of New Westminster's Carnegie Free Library, it is easy to see that what Edwin Sait designed was a Victorian Palladian structure of great charm. Although the library was finished in 1904, a shortage of books meant that it did not open until 1906. Closed in 1958, Sait's fine building was, unfortunately, demolished in 1960.

Survivors

The only two buildings on Columbia Street to survive the Great Fire of 1898 are the three-storey Guichon Block (1873) and the four-storey Burr Block (1892). The buildings stand side by side on the northwest corner of Fourth and Columbia. Both were designed by G.W. Grant, and both are of brick. The Guichon Block (on the right in the photo) is vaguely Italianate and the Burr Block is Victorian Romanesque.

The Guichon Block started life as the Queen's Hotel. After the 1898 fire, when Laurent Guichon lost his hotel that was farther west on Columbia, he bought the Queen's and, after changing its name, reopened for business. His second Guichon Hotel was remodelled in 1910 to accommodate retail shops on the ground floor and apartments on the upper two floors. The original owner of the Burr Block was W.H. Burr, a schoolteacher turned land speculator. Today both buildings are treasured heritage properties.

Bank of Montreal, Fire Dept. and City Hall. New Westminster, B. C.

Gone But Not Forgotten

The years immediately following the Second World War were not particularly kind to New Westminster. In the name of progress, many wonderful late-19th century buildings were demolished in the late 1940s and the 1950s. Perhaps one of the greatest losses occurred when the 1898 Bank of Montreal building was levelled in 1946 and was replaced by a less-than-inspired *Art Moderne* structure that has neither character nor grace.

The old bank building, seen in the foreground, was designed by Francis Rattenbury, the provincial legislative buildings' architect. The bank was the only Rattenbury-designed building in New Westminster. At the time he had a partner, J.G. Tiarks, a British-trained architect of considerable talent, who was also involved in designing New Westminster's Bank of Montreal.

Their bank building opened on October 4, 1899. The *Columbian* reporter waxed eloquent, saying that "its unique design included the eastern touch of minarets on three corners and a centre dome that protected a stained glass layer underneath." While it took an overheated imagination to see the corner domes as minarets, the building—essentially Victorian Romanesque—was a superb and unique structure.

An interesting historical footnote is that this bank was the site of one of North America's most successful heists. On September 14, 1911, John McNamara and his fellow safecrackers robbed it of $258,800—up to that time Canada's largest bank robbery. While a small amount of gold and cash was recovered, the thieves were never successfully prosecuted.

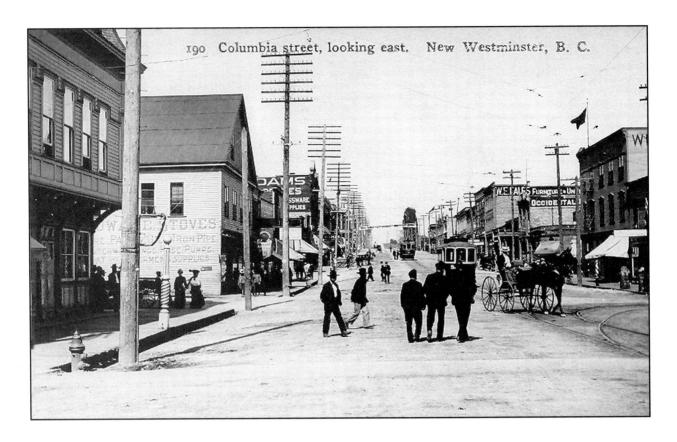

190 Columbia street, looking east. New Westminster, B. C.

Lower Columbia Street

When the fire of September 10, 1898, destroyed most of New Westminster's business district and several blocks of residential properties, the city had fewer than 35 buildings that were of brick or stone: most of the buildings destroyed in the fire were of frame construction.

Although business blocks built after the fire were to be of non-combustible materials, at the lower or west end of Columbia Street owners were allowed to rebuild with wood as quickly as possible, since there was a pressing need to provide accommodation for the homeless. At least two of these frame structures can be seen in Timms' postcard view. And, judging from the picture, jaywalking seems to have been the order of the day!

A Really Big Day

July 23, 1904, was a great day for New Westminster. It was when Lieutenant-Governor Sir Henri-Gustave Joly de Lotbinière officially opened the first bridge across the Fraser River at New Westminster. Unbelievable as it must have been at the time, the bridge that crossed over 2,200 feet of water cost more than $1 million to build. While most of the piers, made of Nelson Island granite, were sunk 69 feet into the riverbed, the pivot pier for the swing span was driven 90 feet into the clay below the river.

As can be seen in Philip Timms' opening-day photo, the bridge had two decks: one to carry road traffic and the other to accommodate rail traffic. The bridge was not only appreciated by the people of New Westminster, but also by those living on the south side of the Fraser who, with the opening of the bridge, finally had easy access to the farmers' market, shops and other attractions in New Westminster.

The Farmers' Market

New Westminster's first farmers' market, at the foot of Church Street facing Lytton Square, opened on November 4, 1892. The square looked more like an unimproved parking lot than anything else, and was used for auctions and as a place where buggies could be left when the horses were stabled in the adjoining livery barn. The market conveniently backed onto a wharf. Fraser Valley farmers got to market in small boats, the scheduled paddlewheelers that ran up and down the river or by using the *Surrey*—the ferry that crossed the river between New Westminster and Brownsville—until 1904, when the bridge at New Westminster opened. The first market has been described as "an old shake-roofed shack." It was one of the first buildings destroyed in the Great Fire of 1898.

Pictured here is the new, much improved market that was built slightly to the east of the original building. With the opening of the Fraser River bridge in 1904, and the opening of B.C. Electric's interurban line to Chilliwack in 1910, the market became increasingly popular and important to New Westminster's life. The market day "specials" on the tramline brought hundreds of buyers and sellers to this venue, and to the Columbia Street shops, theatres and restaurants.

The market burned to the ground on August 17, 1925. It was almost immediately replaced by a three-storey market building that faced onto Columbia Street. It remained at that location until 1947, when the building was sold to David Spencer Limited. It now houses the Army and Navy Department Store.

This Little Piggie Went to Market …

Timms took this wonderful picture in 1904. Two Chinese farmers are driving their pigs along New Westminster's Front Street, just west of Begbie. Since the farmers' market was three blocks east and the men were heading west, it can't be said for sure that the pigs were off to market. The men may have just purchased them at one of T.J. Trapp's auctions that took place in Lytton Square, and could be taking them home to New Westminster's Chinatown, which was west of 8th Street.

The Swanson Block on the corner of Front and Begbie streets housed the Fraser Hotel. Across the street from it was the Sockeye Grocery.

S. S. Transfer, New Westminster, B. C.

A Typical Riverboat

The 264-ton *Transfer* was built for the Canadian Pacific Navigation Company for service on the Fraser River between New Westminster and Chilliwack. When the ship, which carried 120 passengers, was replaced on that run by the *Beaver* in 1898, the *Transfer* ran between New Westminster and Steveston and Ladner at the mouth of the Fraser.

When the CPR bought out Canadian Pacific Navigation in 1901, the *Transfer* became a CP vessel. The ship had a length of 122 feet, a breadth of 24 feet and a draft of only 5.6 feet. It was often said of such shallow draft boats that they could sail on damp grass!

New Westminster, B. C.   Fraser River.

New Westminster's Waterfront

Philip Timms' wonderful picture of the wharves along the Fraser says something about the importance of the river in the lives of Fraser Valley and New Westminster people. Before the arrival of the Canadian Northern Railway (later The Canadian National), and B.C. Electric's Fraser Valley line in 1909–1910, those who lived beyond Cloverdale on the south side of the Fraser were largely dependent on the river for transportation to and from the city and its market. At the same time, of course, the merchants of New Westminster relied heavily on the business generated by the weekly visit of the farmers and their wives.

Pictured midstream is the *Transfer*, and beyond it is the Fraser River bridge. Front Street, with its CPR tracks, can be clearly seen on the left in the photo. In the foreground of this 1905 or 1906 postcard, a freighter is dockside, doubtless loading cases of canned salmon to take to the markets of Europe.

241. Right Wing, Hospital for Insane.
New Westminster, B. C.

The Asylum

In 1876 the contract was let for the Provincial Lunatic Asylum, later known as the Provincial Hospital for the Insane, that was to be built in New Westminster. It was designed by A.J. Smith of Victoria, and built of bricks made in Langley. Even though there were already 35 mentally ill patients being housed in Victoria, the new provincial asylum was built to accommodate only 25 patients. The 125-by-25-foot brick building was ready for occupancy when 20 male and 4 female patients arrived from Victoria on May 17, 1878, accompanied by 3 male keepers and a matron.

The building was enlarged a number of times as the demand for accommodation increased. Whether all those admitted to the mental hospital belonged there is a moot point. The eight patients admitted in 1884, were, for example, suffering from such things as "nervous trouble, masturbation, injury to the head, intemperance, and fright."

By 1900 it was recommended that retarded patients not be housed with the mentally ill, and in 1905 work began on Colony Farm, the first part of a new mental hospital known first as Essondale and later as Riverview. Gradually during the 1920s the mentally ill were moved to the new hospital, leaving the "feeble-minded" in New Westminster. On April 1, 1950, the old Hospital for the Insane became the Woodlands School. It was finally closed on April 3, 2003.

The Royal Columbian

The Royal Columbian Hospital is almost as old as New Westminster itself. In 1862 a public meeting elected a hospital board and agreed that when sufficient funds were available a hospital should be built with the assistance of the city jail's chain gang. The first Royal Columbian—a 30-bed hospital—was built on the corner of 4th and Agnes streets and opened on October 7 to care for men only: women, the incurable and the insane were excluded from care.

In 1889 the Royal Columbian moved to Columbia Street in Sapperton. Its new and spacious three-storey building was designed by Samuel Maclure and Charles Clow, who were in partnership from 1887 until 1891. They were a successful team: Maclure had outstanding design skills and Clow had a strong practical understanding of construction. The new hospital had 50 beds and cost $25,000 to build. Timms' postcard pictures the hospital as it looked in 1905 or 1906.

171

Vancouver

MAIN STREET

Vancouver's Main Street was known in the 1860s as the False Creek Trail. It was built on the recommendation of Colonel Richard Moody of the Royal Engineers to link New Westminster to the government reserve—now Stanley Park—on Burrard Inlet. In 1872 a bridge crossed False Creek, which at the time still extended eastward to Clark Drive.

In 1886 the new city of Vancouver renamed the section of the trail within its city limits Westminster Avenue. To confuse matters further, the False Creek Trail between New Westerminster and Vancouver's 7th Avenue had become known as Westminster Road. The situation improved in 1906 when Westminster Road was renamed Kingsway in honour of King Edward VII.

In 1909, 9th Avenue became Broadway, and there was pressure on the city to rename Westminster Avenue. Some believed that the corner of Broadway and Main was going to become the centre of the metropolitan area; chief among them were the members of what would become the Main Street Improvement Association. Others felt the name "Main Street" would sound less British than "Westminster Avenue," and thus have greater appeal for American investors and real estate men. The outcome of all this was that in 1910, Westminster Avenue became Main Street.

Unfortunately, the hopes and dreams of the Main Street Improvement Association didn't materialize, and Main Street north of Broadway gradually became an avenue of empty lots, industrial properties, streetcar barns, gasworks, B.C. Electric's steam-powered electric generators, cheap hotels, second-hand stores and junkyards—altogether not a pretty sight.

Time, however, has been relatively kind to downtown Main Street. Thanks to modern redevelopment, most of the eyesores have been have been replaced by upscale condominiums and townhouses. And south of Broadway, Mount Pleasant has once again become a good address: a part of the city where a wonderful mix of cultures contributes to a vibrant and exciting lifestyle.

Broadway and Main

Timms titled this postcard, "Waiting for the street car." The streetcar on the left is rounding the corner as it heads westward on 9th Avenue (now Broadway). The second car is heading south on Westminster Avenue (now Main Street) and Timms assumes the people in their summer finery will be boarding that car, once it is through the intersection. On the northwest corner—now occupied by the Lee Building—stood Mount Pleasant Methodist Church, which opened in 1890. Next came a vacant lot, then Herbert Lee's grocery and produce market and one of McDowell, Atkins, and Watson's pharmacies. This picture of Mount Pleasant, Vancouver's first suburb, dates from 1906.

Main and Hastings

Timms' 1905 or 1906 bookmark postcard (opposite page) features a view of Westminster Avenue (now Main Street) looking south beyond Hastings Street. At this time, Main Street looked as good as it was going to for a number of years. The city's shopping and business centre moved westward along Hastings to the CPR's Granville Street fairly quickly, leaving Main Street north of 7th Avenue to rapidly become one of Vancouver's less desirable addresses. In the present century, however, Main Street is well on its way to rehabilitation as more and more condominiums, townhouses and a revitalized Chinatown make it an attractive place to live and work.

Cattle and Councillors

There can't be many cities other than Vancouver that have turned a farmers' market into a city hall. On July 16, 1897, City Council called for tenders "to change the market hall into civic offices ...." The cattle and chickens moved out in 1897 and in 1898 the mayor and council moved in. At this point it's hard to resist making bad jokes about BS and cackling, but on with the story!

Until the move in 1898, the city hall, the police station and the jail were all under one roof in an 1886 Powell Street building. The need for more space for both the civic officials and the police department prompted the city fathers to look for new digs in 1897.

The market hall on Westminster Avenue had been erected by H.F. Keefer to plans drawn up by C.O. Wickenden, who designed many of the city's early buildings, including the present-day Christ Church Cathedral. The red brick supplied for the new two-storey city hall was purchased from Mayor David Oppenheimer's Bowen Island brickyard. As it turned out, the brick had either not been burned hard enough, or the clay used was less than ideal. By the time the contractor was ready to add the second floor, it was realized that with the design they were using, the building of inferior brick could not support a second floor. Wickenden solved the problem by

adding buttresses in the form of matching corner turrets, and placing exceptionally heavy chimneys at intervals along the outside walls. As it happened, the turrets gave the facade added importance and vastly improved the look of the building.

When the new city hall opened in May 1898 all civic offices were on the ground floor. From the day the building opened in 1890 as a market hall, its upper floor had served as a public auditorium, theatre, dance hall and drill hall for the 6th Duke of Connaught's Own Rifles. In June 1910 the mayor's office, the council chamber and other offices were moved upstairs, making the old public auditorium on the second floor a thing of the past.

The building served as city hall until 1929, when the amalgamation of South Vancouver and Point Grey with Vancouver made it necessary to have a much larger one. The Holden Building on Hastings Street was leased, and the old city hall was turned over to the neighbouring public library, which was also badly in need of more space. In 1948 the ornamental cones that topped the corner turrets were removed in the interest of public safety. The central tower had already been removed some years earlier, having succumbed to dry rot. In 1957 City Council called for the demolition of the building, and it was torn down in 1958.

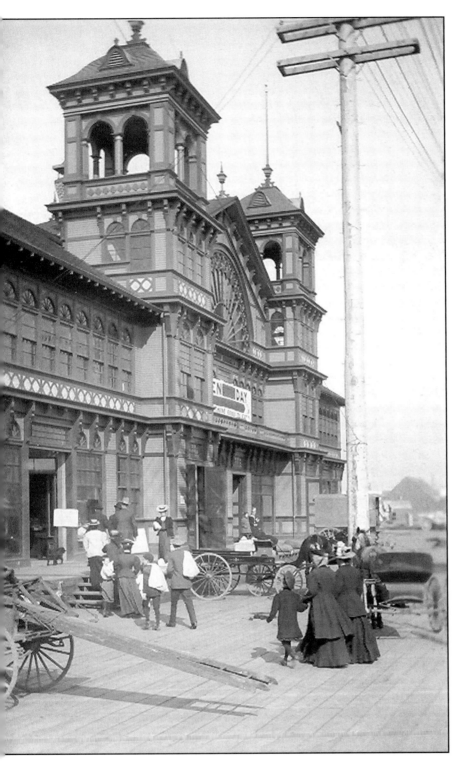

The City Market

Vancouver's original city market was built in 1890. It was an attractive red-brick building that stood on the west side of Main Street (Westminster Avenue) between Hastings and Pender streets. Unfortunately for all who appreciated a market hall where they could buy directly from local farmers, in 1897 the building was appropriated by the mayor and council to become Vancouver's city hall.

Vancouver's citizens looked forward to having a replacement market built as soon as possible. Although a waterfront site between Main Street and Gore Avenue was popularly regarded as the best location, the new city market was built at a cost of $25,000 on a cheaper waterfront site on the south side of False Creek. Designed by W.T. Whiteway, who also designed the Kelly, Douglas Building as well as a number of city schools and the World (Sun) Tower, the new market hall backed onto a large wharf or landing stage, and was in the grand Victorian style popular for exhibition buildings. It could be said of the building that if a little decoration was good, then more was going to be a lot better!

Unfortunately, in time it became apparent that its decoration was the market hall's only appeal. After the initial excitement of opening day, August 15, 1908, the fact that the building was too far from the centre of things proved to be its undoing. There were no stores or retail businesses close by, and a visit to the market inevitably involved a special trip. By the early 1920s the building was no longer used as a market, but had become home to a number of businesses like the Wells' Fish and Fish Ball Company and the Cement Laundry Tray Company. Sadly, Whiteway's rather elegant building burned to the ground in the early morning of November 10, 1925.

The Great Northern Comes to Town

Directly behind the city market stood a large wharf. While it was often used for livestock auctions, its main function was chiefly as a landing stage for small vessels bringing fresh produce to market from Steveston, Ladner, Lulu Island and other points along both the North and South arms of the Fraser River.

Pictured to the west of the wharf in Timms' postcard is a trestle with a swing span crossing the shallow waters of False Creek. It allowed the trains of one of the Great Northern Railway's Canadian subsidiaries, the Vancouver and Eastern Railway, to reach the company's station, which stood on the corner of Pender and Columbia streets. The line, which was built in 1903–04, ran between New Westminster and Vancouver. When the first bridge crossed the Fraser River at New Westminster in 1904, the Vancouver and Eastern Railway connected directly with another of the Great Northern's subsidiaries, the 1901 Vancouver, New Westminster and Yukon Railway, which ran from the south bank of the Fraser River to the international border, where its tracks met those of its American parent company. It wasn't until 1908 that the company's Canadian lines became an integral part of the Great Northern Railway (now the Burlington Northern Santa Fe).

The Pender Street station continued to be used until the Union Station built by the Great Northern and Union Pacific railways—both controlled by James J. Hill, a Canadian by birth—opened in 1917 on the newly reclaimed flats at the east end of False Creek. When there was no longer a need for the trestle and its span, they were torn down.

Vancouver

GETTING IT WHOLESALE

For much of its history Vancouver has been handicapped in the race to become a significant manufacturing centre by the enterprise that created it, namely, the Canadian Pacific Railway (CPR). Major Canadian markets for manufactured goods have always been east of the Rockies, and because the CPR imposed discriminatory freight rates for goods moving east from British Columbia, it was impossible for Vancouver to compete successfully as an industrial centre. The logic justifying the railway's higher rates for goods moving eastward was the fact that it cost more to build the rail line through the mountains than it did to build it anywhere else in Canada.

While Vancouver was effectively out of the running in the race to become a vital manufacturing hub, its geographic location did give it great potential to become an important wholesale distribution centre. Being Canada's "Gateway to the Orient" meant that much of the tea, coffee, spices and other exotic treasures of the Far East came into the country by way of Water Street's wholesale houses and customs brokers. Because the properties along the north side of Water Street backed onto CPR trackage, most of the firms dealing in either groceries or produce were located on the north side of the street. Even though Water Street only extends for three blocks, in 1910 it was home to 17 wholesale grocers and produce merchants.

The street also attracted wholesale clothing and dry-goods merchants, ships' chandlers and sail makers, raw fur dealers and suppliers for the upcoast fish canneries. Manufacturers' agents for eastern Canadian, British and American firms that provided heavy equipment and other machinery to coastal and Interior logging and mining camps had offices on Water Street. As well, stevedores and seasonally unemployed loggers lived in the street's 15 hotels, each of which, with one exception, had its own bar. The exception was the Temperance Hotel at 301 Water Street.

By the 1960s limited space and the rising cost of real estate made it necessary for many Water Street wholesale houses to move to Burnaby and beyond. At the same time, developers had rediscovered Gastown, which centred on Water Street; they refurbished its old, often attractive buildings, giving them a new lease on life as shops, restaurants, galleries and offices. To give the developers their due, with every passing year Water Street is becoming much more upscale and, in its heritage setting, providing tourists and locals alike with a positive experience of "early Vancouver."

At the North End of Richards

Timms' view looks northward down Richards to the Kelly, Douglas and Company building. Robert Kelly and Frank Douglas established their wholesale grocery business in April 1896. It grew quickly, and when gold was discovered in the Yukon in 1898 their firm became actively involved in catering to the needs of the many would-be gold seekers heading north. While Seattle's merchants profited most from the rush to the Klondike, Vancouver's Kelly, Douglas and Company competed successfully and gained a sound reputation for reliable customer service all over B.C. and the Yukon.

During their years together, Kelly usually stayed in Vancouver while Douglas travelled throughout B.C. and the Yukon, establishing contacts that were to assure the firm's future as one of Canada's premier wholesale houses. Success came in part from the fact that Kelly, Douglas was not elitist: one man's dollar was as good as another's, as long as it was spent at Kelly, Douglas!

Frank Douglas didn't live long enough to enjoy the fruits of his labour. Returning to Vancouver from the Yukon, where he had been writing up orders for the firm, he sailed from Skagway aboard the CPR's *Islander*. The ship left Skagway on August 14, 1901, with a crew of 62 and 110 passengers. Not far from Juneau, at 2:16 a.m. on August 15, the ship struck an iceberg and sank in 365 feet of water in 16 minutes. Frank Douglas was one of the 42 aboard who were drowned.

Robert Kelly was fortunate in finding a new partner in 1904 in the person of Edward Douglas, Frank's older brother. While Edward knew nothing about wholesale groceries when he joined the firm, he was already a successful and wealthy businessman who brought his many valuable skills to the partnership.

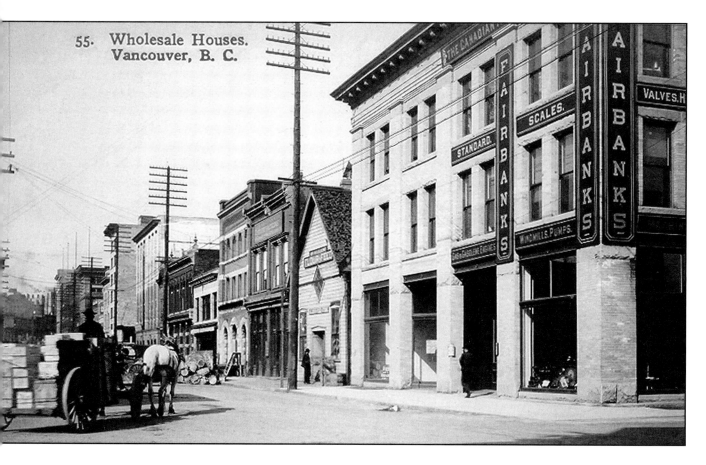

55. Wholesale Houses.
Vancouver, B. C.

A Less Hurried Life

A postcard from the summer of 1906 pictures the Canadian Fairbanks Company's new home on the northwest corner of Water and Abbott streets. The building was erected at a cost of $50,000 for McLennan, McFeely and Company, the city's leading hardware wholesalers of the time. Just why "Mc & Mc" put up the building is not known: perhaps it was as an investment, or in anticipation of their own future need for an additional warehouse. In 1910 Canadian Fairbanks was advertising itself as "the largest machinery and mill supply house in Canada." Their heavy-duty equipment was sold under the Fairbanks-Morse trademark.

The hip-roofed building next door to Canadian Fairbanks was the premises of Allen Fredericks, flour and feed merchant. The 16-by-30 foot structure had been erected by the Methodists in 1876 as Granville's or Gastown's first church. While it was Methodist in name, it had a board of trustees made up of four Anglicans, two Methodists and one Presbyterian. Services for all denominations were held in the building. By 1887 the various denominations each had their own churches, and the building was sold.

The dray slowly rounding the corner onto Water Street appears to be carrying produce, though one gets the feeling that it isn't going to be all that fresh by the time it finally reaches its destination.

"Commercial Awakening"

Fortunately, Philip Timms had an eye for the unusual photographic shot. This view looks westward toward the intersection of Water, Cordova and Richards streets. The year in which the postcard was produced was probably 1909.

The nine-storey building on the left was the 1908 addition to David Spencer's department store, which fronted on Hastings Street. In time, Spencer's fashionable roof garden, with its commanding view of the harbour and beyond, was atop the building pictured.

Kelly, Douglas and Company's premises take up all of the right-hand side of the card. While Kelly, Douglas began life as a wholesale grocer, it soon became much more than that. Within its walls many of the Nabob products it marketed were produced. At nine storeys, the company's new building was the tallest in Vancouver when it opened in 1906. The structure, designed by W.T. Whiteway, was built of brick and faced with dressed brick and sandstone. Amazingly, the structure was framed entirely of timber. At the building's lowest level are supporting wood columns of 18-by-18 inches. Each succeeding floor has slightly more slender columns until those at the top floor are only 8-by-8 inches. A huge addition was added to the west of the original building in 1910.

Kelly, Douglas originally used "Nabob" as the name of one of the quality teas it first imported in 1896 from Ceylon (now Sri Lanka). In 1905 the company registered the name and it became the brand name for most of the products marketed by the firm. The word is an English corruption of the Urdu term *nawwāb*. In the days of the Mogul empire, a *nawwāb* was a deputy who served as governor of a town or district in India. Such a person, almost by definition, would have been someone of great wealth and discerning taste. As the company advertised, "Nabob on the label

means quality on the table." The company did very well, recording gross sales of $5.5 million in 1913, and $10 million in the Depression year of 1937.

In 1948 Kelly, Douglas moved from Water Street to 4700 Kingsway in Burnaby. The Burnaby site was eventually sold to Cambridge Shopping Centres, the developers of Metrotown. Kelly, Douglas and

Company indirectly became a subsidiary of the George Weston group in 1958.

The Water Street building is now known as the Landing and is a fashionable mix of boutiques, restaurants and offices. Its proximity to the cruise ship docks makes it attractive to tourists as well as to locals.

Vancouver

AND SO WE CLOSE

While a number of local photographers were producing picture postcards during the Golden Age of Postcards, there is no doubt that one of them—Philip Timms—was unique. While he was happy to make money, Timms saw a larger purpose in what he was doing as he took pictures of people at play, at home and at work, and of the settings in which they lived their day-to-day lives.

In 1911 Timms said of his pictures, "Twenty-five years from now these pictures will be a valuable … record of the city's history." It didn't take long for him to feel disappointment. In 1936, the year of Vancouver's golden jubilee, he complained that "city officials [are] too busy living Vancouver's life at its fiftieth anniversary to commemorate its history."

Timms mastered the photographer's art, and left a record of the city's youthful years in a collection of over 3,000 photographs. Of that number, he published over 1,200 as picture postcards. We end by offering a sampling of other cards and subjects as a kind of reminder that there is still much more of Philip Timms' work to be seen.

ST. ANDREW PRESBYTERIAN CHURCH, 1904.

St. Andrew's Presbyterian
Philip Timms photographed many of the city's churches. Among them was St. Andrew's Presbyterian Church, which stood on the corner of Richards and Georgia streets. Designed by William Blackmore and built in Carpenter Gothic style, this large and impressive church opened May 25, 1890. Interestingly, Blackmore also designed Wesley Methodist Church, which stood on the corner of Burrard and Georgia. After church union in 1925, these two churches combined their congregations and went on to build St. Andrew's Wesley on Burrard Street in 1931-33.

A Day's Outing

Timms had a lot of time for picnics: he loved anything that gave him an excuse to be outdoors, and he never tired of producing postcards that pictured people at play. Here a father and daughter are carrying the family picnic hamper down to the excursion steamer that will take them to Bowen Island and back for only 50¢ per person.

Camping on Howe Sound

Philip Timms was an active member of the Vancouver Natural History Society. This picture was taken on the Dominion Day weekend in 1911, and may be a Timms family photo. By the look of the camping equipment, roughing it was certainly the order of the day.

WISHING YOU A *Merry Christmas* AND A *Happy New Year.*

921. A January Skate.
Vancouver, B. C.

St. Paul's Hospital

Vancouver's St. Paul's Hospital opened on November 24, 1894. It was founded and staffed by the Roman Catholic Sisters of Charity of Providence, a French-Canadian order whose mother house was in Montreal. When St. Paul's was built, its location was considered remote: it was at the south end of the Burrard Street trail. The frame structure was replaced by a new brick building in 1913. Note the overprint—many of Timms' postcards were used as Christmas cards.

"A Punny Thing"

Timms loved puns and could not resist entitling this fish market card "A January Skate." One of the more interesting things about the postcard is the fishmonger. There he is, dressed in a suit, vest and tie, working all day with smelly, messy fish. His special cuffs and heavy apron are all that suggest he was working in a fish market.

Glory Days

Before the Great War, the West End was home to the city's elite. All was serene until April 28, 1909, when the CPR put its first 120 lots in Shaughnessy Heights up for sale by auction. The lots in Shaughnessy (derisively referred to as "CPR Heaven" by those who chose not to bid on lots or could not afford to do so) were all sold in three hours. Over 1,000 attended the auction, and lots sold for between $1,000 and $4,150. Many onlookers thought the prices were beyond reason. Virtually overnight, however, the West End was no longer the city's most fashionable address.

Cedar Cottage

Cedar Cottage was only just becoming a residential suburb when Timms created this postcard in 1902 or 1903. The road in front of the fence is now Knight Street, and the trees at the top of the hill mark the location of what was known for many years as Buffalo Park, now known by its original name, Clark Park. The break in the trees marks the road allowance for either East 17th or 18th Avenue.

SELECTED BIBLIOGRAPHY

Books and Articles

Brown, Ron. *The Train Doesn't Stop Here Anymore.* Peterborough, ON: Broadway Press, 1991.

Davies, Bill. *From Sourdough to Superstore: the Kelly, Douglas Story.* Vancouver: Kelly, Douglas and Company, 1990.

Delgado, James P. *Waterfront.* Vancouver: Stanton, Atkins & Dosil, 2005.

F.G. Architectural and Planning Consultants. *City of North Vancouver Heritage Inventory.* North Vancouver: City of North Vancouver, 1949.

Hacking, N.R. and W. Kaye Lamb. *The Princess Story: a Century and a Half of West Coast Shipping.* Vancouver: Mitchell Press, 1974.

Kidd, Thomas. *History of Lulu Island and Occasional Poems.* Vancouver: Wrigley Printing Company, 1927.

Martin, J. Edward. *The Railway Stations of Western Canada.* White Rock: Studio E Martin, 1980.

Matches, Alex. *It Began With a Ronald—A Pictorial History of Vancouver's Firefighting Equipment.* Vancouver: Mitchell Press, 1974.

Mattison, David. *Camera Workers: The British Columbia Photographic Directory, 1858–1950.* Victoria: Camera Workers Press, 1985.

Mills, Edward and Warren Sommer. *Vancouver Architecture, 1886–1914,* Volumes I and II. Vancouver: Environment Canada, 1975.

Morton, D.M. *Early History of Port Moody.* Surrey: Hancock House, 1987.

Mullan, M. *Britannia—The Story of a British Columbia Mine.* Britannia Beach: British Columbia Museum of Mining, undated.

Rees-Thomas, David M. *Timber Down the Capilano.* Victoria: The BC Railway Historical Association, 1927.

Ross, J.L. *Richmond: Child of the Fraser.* Richmond: Richmond '79 Centennial Society and the Corporation of the Township of Richmond, 1979.

Snyders, Tom and Jennifer O'Rourke. *Namely Vancouver: A Hidden History of Vancouver Place Names.* Vancouver: Arsenal Pulp Press, 2001.

Swan, Joe. *A Century of Service: The Vancouver Police, 1886–1986.* Vancouver: Vancouver Police Historical Society and the Vancouver Centennial Museum, 1986.

Town, F.A. *The Lively Ghost of Howe Sound.* Port Coquitlam: Bookus Press, 2000.

———. *Before the Road Came.* Port Coquitlam: Bookus Press, 2004.

Vancouver Annual. Vancouver: Editorial Department—Progress Club, undated.

Vancouver: The Golden Years: 1900–1910, Vancouver: Vancouver Museum and Planetarium Association, 1971.

Walker, Elizabeth. *Street Names of Vancouver.* Vancouver: Vancouver Historical Society, 1999.

Wolf, Jim. *Early History of Barnet.* Burnaby: unpublished and undated manuscript.

———. *Royal City, 1858–1960.* Surrey, BC: Heritage House, 2005.

———. *The North Pacific Lumber Company, 1889–1914.* Burnaby: unpublished and undated manuscript.

Yesaki, Mitsuo and Harold and Kathy Steves. *Steveston Cannery Row.* Richmond: self-published, 1998.

Websites

"A Short History of the North Shore." www.cherrybouton.com/nshistory

Calderone, John A. "Fire Apparatus Past and Present." http://firefightercentral.com/history/fire_apparatus_past_and_present.htm

Kingslake, Rudolf. "Gundlach." 1974. A History of the Rochester, N.Y. Camera and Lens Companies www.nwmangum.com/Kodak/Rochester

Leggat, Robert. "Louis Jacques Mande Daguerre." 2000. www.rleggat.com/photohistory/history

———. "Joseph Nicéphore Niépce," *A History of Photography* www.rleggat.com/photohistory/history/niepce.htm

Niederman, Rob. "Henry Clay Cameras and the Dry Plate Revolution." 2006.

———. "The Korona Hand Camera, 1895." 2003. http://antiquewoodcameras.com/milburn.htm

Resnick, Mason. *Black & White Film Processing: The Twelve-Step Program."* Photographer's Tool Kit, 2004. www.photogs.com/bwworld/bwfilmdev.html

The Fox Talbot Museum, "William Henry Fox Talbot." www.r-cube.co.uk/fox-talbot/history.html

Vancouver Public Library. *"British Columbia: Through the Camera Lens of Philip Timms."* Vancouver: Vancouver Public Library. www.vpl.ca

PHOTOGRAPHY AND PHILIP TIMMS

Photography came into being between 1827 and 1839, when three men independently discovered the photographic process. In France, Joseph Nicéphore Niépce created the first recognizable photographic image in 1826 or 1827. He teamed up with Louis Daguerre in 1829, forming a partnership that lasted until Niépce's death in 1833. After that Daguerre continued to experiment on his own and produced his first "daguerreotype" in 1837. In England, William Fox Talbot made the earliest surviving latent negative on paper in 1835, and went on to create the "calotype" in 1841. The calotype used paper sheets coated with silver chloride that been set with a potassium bromide solution. His process was the first to produce a negative image that could be reproduced any number of times.

Both the French and English processes had drawbacks. While the daguerreotype produced a very clear image, it was a "once only" process, and expensive to boot. The calotype, on the other hand, was capable of unlimited reproduction, but the resulting images, created from paper negatives, were not particularly sharp.

In 1848 Frederick Scott Archer, an Englishman, developed the collodion process that made everyday photography practical for the first time. Archer knew that collodion—a flammable liquid created by cellulose nitrate and ether—produced a transparent, waterproof slick when poured onto a glass plate. He also discovered that when the treated plate was plunged into a bath of silver nitrate, the collodion was turned into

The Gundlach-Manhattan Camera

Philip Timms' favourite camera was a 1902 Gundlach-Manhattan Optical Company camera. It was designed to use either glass plate or sheet film. Timms preferred using the 5-by-7-inch glass plates to create his negatives. Gundlach-Manhattan, like so many other companies in the evolving camera and film industry, was located in Rochester, New York.

Physically the camera is both attractive and practical. Its dimensions when closed are 8.25-by-8.25-by-4-inches, making it easily portable. The camera's case is covered in black, pebble-grain morocco leather, and it has a leather handle.

The front drops open on a metal hinge to reveal an interior of polished red mahogany and a cherry-red leather bellows. The lens plate slides forward along a metal focussing rail. All the hardware is nickel-plated brass. Its lens was lost some time before the camera was donated to the Vancouver Museum.

photo-sensitive silver iodide. The "wet plate" so produced could then be exposed in a camera, and developed in either a darkroom or a developing tent. The importance of Archer's discoveries was that they allowed identical prints to be made in quantities. While the collodion wet-plate process required a developing time of only a few seconds, prints could only be made before the collodion solution dried, that is, in about five minutes on a warm day.

Dr. Richard Maddox, an English physician and enthusiastic photographer, looked for a substitute for collodion: the ether used in the wet-plate process was affecting his health adversely. In 1871 he suggested a dry-plate process in which a light-sensitive mixture of cadmium bromide in silver nitrate could be coated on a glass plate in a gelatin emulsion. By 1880 factory-made glass/gelatin dry plates were widely available to photographers: Philip Timms used 3,000 of them! Glass plates were used until the late 1920s, even though George Eastman had invented and produced roll film and his first simple Kodak box camera in 1888; new ideas were sometimes slow to catch on.

For example, it was not until the 1890s that the self-encased, folding bellows, dry-plate negative cameras were accepted by the general public, even though they were relatively easy to use, readily portable and able to produce instantaneous snapshots of street scenes or special events. Such a camera, however, was just what Philip Timms wanted, and in 1902 he purchased one produced by the Gundlach-Manhattan Optical Company of Rochester, New York, the leading seller of dry-plate cameras at the time. Timms' camera, minus its lens, is now in the collection of the Vancouver Museum. While Timms had a first-rate camera that made it possible for him to control focus, depth of field and the sharpness of his photographic images, above all else it was his developing skills that gave his pictures their unique quality and appeal.

It is often assumed that because a photograph is old, it is going to be sepia toned. Such is not the case: most old photographs that are now "brownish" were originally black-and-white photos. Hurried or sloppy developing and printing very often caused them to fade to rather unattractive brown tones over the years. However, the best photographers, like Philip Timms, intentionally looked for a signature tonal quality that would not only identify their work as unique, but best preserve it for posterity.

Timms tonal quality resulted from the types of paper he used—Velox and Azo, both produced by Kodak—and his unique developing solution, which included gold salts rather than silver nitrate, thereby strengthening the warm quality of his images. As well, the great care he took in both developing and printing his postcards did much to assure the lasting clarity and increasing value of his work.

INDEX